MACMILLAN READERS

INTERMEDIATE LEVEL

STEPHEN COLBOURN

King Arthur
and the
Knights of the Round Table

D0924447

MACMILLAN

MACMILLAN READERS

INTERMEDIATE LEVEL

Founding Editor: John Milne

The Macmillan Readers provide a choice of enjoyable reading materials for learners of English. The series is published at six levels – Starter, Beginner, Elementary, Pre-intermediate, Intermediate and Upper.

Level Control
Information, structure and vocabulary are controlled to suit the students' ability at each level.

The number of words at each level:

Starter	about 300 basic words
Beginner	about 600 basic words
Elementary	about 1100 basic words
Pre-intermediate	about 1400 basic words
Intermediate	about 1600 basic words
Upper	about 2200 basic words

Vocabulary
Some difficult words and phrases in this book are important for understanding the story. Some of these words are explained in the story, some are shown in the pictures, and others are marked with a number like this: ...³. Words with a number are explained in the Glossary at the end of the book.

Answer Keys
Answer Keys for the *Points for Understanding* and *Exercises* sections can be found at www.macmillanenglish.com/readers

Contents

A Note About These Stories 4

A Picture Dictionary 6

The People in These Stories 7

1 The Coming of Arthur 9

2 The Sword in the Stone 15

3 Excalibur 19

4 Queen Guinevere 22

5 Merlin and Nimuë 27

6 Sir Gawain and the Green Knight 32

7 The Chapel Perilous 39

8 Tristram and Iseult 46

9 Percivale and Lancelot 56

10 The Siege Perilous 62

11 The Quest for the Holy Grail 66

12 The Breaking of the Round Table 70

13 The Passing of Arthur 77

Points for Understanding 81

Glossary 84

Exercises 89

A Note About These Stories

The stories of King Arthur are more than a thousand years old. They are stories; they are not history. But, history records the name of a war leader *Artorius* who lived around the year 500 AD. Perhaps the name 'Artorius' became 'Arthur' in the stories of King Arthur.

The Romans ruled Britain between 43 AD and 410 AD. Then, after the Romans left, there was no longer one government in the country. For centuries, there were many small kingdoms in Britain. The rulers of these kingdoms were warriors[1] or war leaders. These British leaders fought invaders[2] who came from the countries across the North Sea and the first stories of King Arthur date from about this time. But the most famous stories came from a later period.

The Roman Empire[3] became weak after the year 400 AD. During the next century, many different people moved across Europe from east to west. People from northern Germany and Scandinavia invaded Britain and drove the British people into the western and northern lands of Britain. These Anglo-Saxon invaders named the country Angleland, or England. Many years later, they became the English people and their language became English.

For two hundred years after this, Vikings from Scandinavia attacked[4] the coast of Britain. They also invaded France and mixed with Celts and Bretons. In France, the Vikings were called Normans – north men. Soon, these people no longer spoke German or Scandinavian. They spoke French and in 1066 AD, the Normans invaded Britain.

Over a century later, French poets and storytellers told the stories of King Arthur. They told the stories in the French language. Then, in the 14th century, poets and storytellers began to tell the stories in English. In these stories, a young man called Arthur became King of Britain. Arthur called the best warriors to his court[5] at Castle Camelot. The warriors, or knights, sat at a round table in the hall of the castle.

A magician[6] named Merlin helped Arthur to rule the land. These stories are about the Knights of the Round Table and their adventures. The stories describe how a good knight must behave. A good knight was chivalrous[7] and polite. He was a warrior and a powerful member of society. A knight supported his king and fought for honour, truth and justice[8]. He also went on quests[9]. He might have to kill an enemy or a dragon. Perhaps he had to save a young woman. Or he might have to find something that was holy or valuable. When he had done these things, his quest was completed.

Stories about Arthur have been retold many times. They are the subject of books, plays, films, operas and poems. In *The Lord of the Rings* and *The Hobbit* by J. R. R. Tolkien, Gandalf the Wizard is based on Merlin the Magician. In the *Star Wars* films, the Jedi Knights are based on the Knights of the Round Table.

A Picture Dictionary

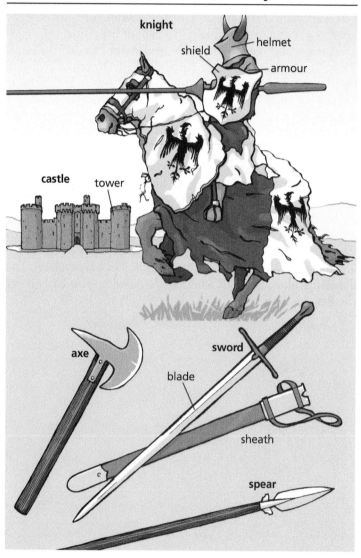

knight

shield
helmet
armour

castle
tower

axe
sword
blade
sheath
spear

The People in These Stories

Name	*Role in the stories*
Merlin the Magician	*a powerful wizard, guardian of Arthur*
Uther Pendragon	*King of Winchester*
Gorloïs	*King of Cornwall*
Igrayne	*Queen of Cornwall*
Morgana Le Fey	*a sorceress, half-sister of Arthur and mother of Mordred*
Arthur	*son of Uther Pendragon and Igrayne, King of Britain*
Ector	*an old knight, foster father of Arthur*
Kay	*son of Ector*
Bedivere	*the oldest knight of the Round Table*
Lancelot	*the bravest knight and Champion of Camelot, also lover of Queen Guinevere and father of Galahad*
Gawain	*the greatest knight*
Guinevere	*daughter of Leodogran and wife of Arthur*
Leodogran	*King of Cameliard*
Nimuë	*a sorceress and companion of Morgana*
The Green Knight	*Master of the Green Chapel*
Tristram	*Champion of King Mark of Cornwall, lover of Iseult the Fair*
Percivale	*the purest knight, afterwards guardian of the Grail Chapel*
Galahad	*the perfect knight, son of Lancelot, who achieves the Quest for the Holy Grail*
Meliot	*the wounded knight*
Gilbert	*the Black Knight*
Lady Gilbert	*a sorceress, also called Hellawes*
Elaine	*the Fair Maid of Astolat*
Iseult the Fair	*daughter of the King and Queen of Ireland, wife of King Mark and lover of Tristram*
Mark	*King of Cornwall*
Gurman	*King of Ireland*

The People in These Stories

Name	Role in the stories
Isaud	*Queen of Ireland*
Marhault	*Champion of Ireland*
Brangwain	*servant of Iseult the Fair*
Iseult of the White Hands	*wife of Tristram*
Kurwenal	*servant of Tristram*
Gareth	*a knight of Camelot*
Naciens	*the holy hermit of Carbonek*
Blanchefleur	*daughter of King Pelles and mother of Galahad, afterwards wife of Percivale*
King Pelles	*the wounded king, the old Grail Knight*
Bors	*a knight of Camelot*
Agravaine	*a knight of Camelot*
Mordred	*the evil knight, son of Arthur and Morgana Le Fey*
Lohengrin	*son of Percivale and Blanchefleur, also called Loherangrin or the Swan Knight*

1

The Coming of Arthur

Merlin the Magician and King Uther Pendragon

It was a time of war in Britain. There was much fighting and killing. There were many small kingdoms in Britain and each kingdom had its own king. But no king was strong enough to rule all the land. There was no peace in Britain and the people suffered.

Merlin the Magician spoke to the people. 'One king will come,' he said. 'All the land will become one kingdom. And one king will rule in one land. There will be peace at last.'

But who was this king? Perhaps it was Uther Pendragon, the King of Winchester. Uther was a strong king with a large army. He ruled most of southern Britain. Only the land of Cornwall, to the far west, had a king as powerful as Uther. The King of Cornwall was named Gorloïs.

King Uther spoke to Merlin the Magician. 'I will go to Cornwall,' said Uther. 'I will make peace with King Gorloïs. I will marry one of his daughters and we will have a son. Then our son will be King of all Britain.'

Merlin was silent. He looked at King Uther. Uther was short but he had a strong body. His hair and eyes were as black as the feathers of a raven[10]. Uther spoke loudly and roughly. Men were afraid of him because he was always angry. Uther rode a great warhorse and he carried a heavy sword. He could kill a man with one blow[11] of his sword.

Merlin was the opposite of Uther. Merlin was tall, but he was not strong. He did not carry a sword. Merlin's hair was as white as the feathers of a swan[12], but he was not an old man.

No one knew where Merlin came from. Some men said that Merlin came out of the west, from across the sea.

Merlin spoke quietly and said few words. But everyone listened to him when he spoke, because Merlin was wise and clever.

'Tell me, magician,' said Uther. 'Can you look into the future? Can you tell me – will my son be King of all Britain?'

Merlin was silent. His eyes were the colour of the clear blue sky. He did not look at the king; he looked far away. And there was sadness in Merlin's eyes when he spoke.

'Yes, Sire[13],' said the magician softly. 'Your son will be King of all Britain. But the unmarried daughter of King Gorloïs is very young. She is only a child.'

Uther Pendragon's face became bright with joy. 'Bring horses!' he shouted to his men. 'We will ride to Cornwall.'

Gorloïs – King of Cornwall

After many days, King Uther came to the land of Cornwall. He rode to Tintagel Castle, where King Gorloïs lived with his wife, Igrayne. The castle was built of black stone and stood on a high cliff above a dark sea.

'King Uther, you are welcome!' said Gorloïs. 'Eat and drink. We will be friends.'

So Uther and Gorloïs sat in the castle hall and ate and drank. King Gorloïs was an old, grey-haired man, but his wife, Igrayne, was young and very beautiful. Her hair was the colour of gold.

As soon as Uther saw Igrayne, he looked at no one else. He drank more and more wine and his face became red. He stared at Queen Igrayne. But she would not look at Uther. She lowered her eyes. King Gorloïs looked angrily at his guest.

'Tell me, lady,' said Uther to Igrayne. 'How many children do you have?'

'Three,' answered Queen Igrayne. 'My two older daughters are married. My youngest daughter is three years old. Her name is Morgana.'

Uther drank more wine. 'I can give you a son,' he said.

When King Gorloïs heard these words, he stood up and put his hand on his sword. 'Uther Pendragon! Leave my house now,' he shouted, 'and never return!'

Uther stood up slowly. 'I will leave,' he said to Gorloïs, 'but I will return with an army.'

And, so, King Uther made war against King Gorloïs. In October, Uther's army attacked Tintagel Castle. But Uther could not take the castle – it was too strong.

Igrayne – Queen of Cornwall

'I do not want Tintagel Castle,' Uther said to Merlin. 'I want Queen Igrayne. She will be my wife! Winter is coming and my men have little food. I will take the army back to Winchester. But first, I must have Igrayne. Help me, Merlin. And I will do anything that you say.'

'Tell your men to leave,' Merlin said. 'Tell them to move east, back towards Winchester. But tell them not to go far. They must wait in the woods. King Gorloïs will see that your men are leaving. He will come out of the castle and follow your army. Then you will go inside the castle and visit Igrayne.'

'The castle guards will kill me,' said Uther.

'I will protect[14] you,' said Merlin. 'I will use magic. I will cast a spell[15] and I will change you. For one night, I will give you the face and body of Gorloïs. But you must do one thing for me.'

'What do you want?' asked Uther Pendragon.

11

Uther Pendragon's promise to Merlin

'Igrayne will have a child,' said Merlin. 'You will give that child to me.'

'Yes,' said Uther. 'I will give you the child.'

So Uther gave orders to his men: 'Move away from the castle. Move back to the woods.'

The men walked away to the east, back towards Winchester. But they did not go far. Before night came, Uther's men stopped. They waited in the woods.

But Uther did not go with his men. He and Merlin hid in a circle of tall stones and waited. The king and the magician watched the gates of the castle. At last, the gates opened. King Gorloïs came out with his men and they followed Uther's army.

Merlin spoke words of magic. He cast a spell. Slowly, the shape of Uther's face and body changed until he looked like an old, grey-haired man. Uther had become Gorloïs!

Uther rode his horse to the gates of Tintagel Castle. 'Open the gates!' he ordered the guards. 'I will go to the Queen.'

Uther Pendragon went to the bedchamber of Queen Igrayne. And that night, there was a great storm. The wind blew from the sea and lightning lit the black walls of the castle. The sound of thunder was loud, but the sounds of battle were louder. The armies of Uther and Gorloïs were fighting with swords and axes. Igrayne cried out as she slept.

In the morning, Uther was gone. Igrayne went to the eastern walls of the castle and saw her husband's army returning. But King Uther's men were behind the army of Gorloïs and they were carrying her husband's body on a shield. King Gorloïs was dead. He had been killed in the battle and his body was covered in blood from many wounds[16].

Then Uther entered Tintagel Castle as himself and Igrayne became his wife.

The birth of Arthur

Uther stayed at Tintagel until the middle of the next year. On Midsummer's Day, Igrayne gave birth[17] to a son. But she did not give her son a name.

That night, Merlin came to the castle. Uther and Igrayne were holding their newborn son. Igrayne's daughter, Morgana, was with them.

Merlin did not speak to Uther and Igrayne. He took the baby boy and looked at him. 'I name you, Arthur,' he said.

'Give me my son!' Igrayne cried. But Uther remembered his promise and did not stop the magician. Merlin took the boy and went away.

Igrayne wept all night and all day. Slowly her sadness and pain made her go mad. She ran to the western walls of the castle and threw herself into the sea.

Morgana Le Fey and the death of Uther

Uther and his men left the castle. He took Igrayne's daughter, Morgana, with him. When he reached the town of Glastonbury he found a nunnery[18] with high walls. There, holy women – or nuns – lived and never went outside.

'Morgana will be a nun,' Uther said. 'She will stay inside the nunnery walls. No man shall see her face again.'

Then Uther returned to Winchester. He was now king in the south of Britain. There was peace in the land for a time, but Uther had many enemies.

One enemy, who lived in the north, sent a servant to work in the king's kitchen at Winchester. The servant put poison into King Uther's wine. Uther drank the wine and died at the table in the great hall of his castle.

Merlin promises a New King

For fifteen summers and winters, there was no king in the south and the people suffered because there was no order in the land. Then, one night, Merlin came secretly to Winchester. He went to Winchester Cathedral – the great church in the town – and spoke to the archbishop[19].

'Tell all the people to come to the cathedral on Sunday,' he said.

On Sunday, the knights and the people of Winchester came to the cathedral. They prayed for peace and a good king. And while they were praying, they heard a sound like music outside the cathedral.

The people went outside. In the field by the church, they saw a large stone. The stone was half as big as a man. A bright, metal sword was standing in the stone. The people could see only the handle of the sword.

The archbishop looked at the stone and the sword. Words were written on the stone in gold letters:

THE MAN WHO PULLS THIS SWORD FROM
THE STONE IS THE TRUE KING OF ALL
BRITAIN.

Then one by one, the men tried to pull the sword from the stone. All the knights of Winchester tried, but they all failed. The sword did not move.

'The true king is not here today,' said the archbishop. 'I will send messengers through all the lands of Britain. Soon, everyone will know about this sword. Anyone who wants to pull the sword out of the stone must come here at Christmas. On New Year's Day, we will have a contest. We will see who can draw the sword from the stone.'

2

The Sword in the Stone

The contest at Winchester

All the knights of Britain came to gather at Winchester. They put their tents in the fields near the cathedral. It was winter and very cold so the men lit fires to keep warm.

Sir Ector was an old, brave and honest knight. He came to Winchester with his two sons – Kay and Arthur. The three men rode their horses towards the cathedral. It was New Year's Day and they were going to the gathering of the knights.

Kay was eighteen years old and ready to become a knight. But only a king can give a man this title. And there was no king in the land.

Arthur was nearly sixteen years old. He did not look like his brother, Kay. Kay was dark-haired. But Arthur had fair hair, which was almost the colour of gold. Arthur was taller and stronger than his older brother.

Kay stopped his horse. Then he put his hand on his sheath and felt for his sword. But the sheath was empty. 'I have forgotten my sword,' he said to Arthur. 'I helped Father to put on his armour but I forgot to put my own sword in my sheath.'

'I will ride back to our tent,' said Arthur. 'The knights are gathering near the cathedral. Go there. I will fetch your sword and bring it to you.'

'Ride quickly,' said Kay.

So Arthur rode his horse back across the field. Then, in the middle of the field, he saw the stone and the sword. The bright sunshine shone on the sword.

'No one is using this sword,' Arthur thought. 'I will borrow it for my brother Kay.' Then the young man pulled the sword from the stone and took it to his brother.

Arthur takes the Sword

Arthur did not know why the sword was in the stone. But Kay knew about the sword and the other knights knew too. They all gathered around Kay and Arthur.

'Who gave you this sword?' asked a knight. 'What are you doing with it?'

'Arthur, this sword does not belong to you,' said Sir Ector. 'Put the sword back in the stone. The sword belongs to the true king.'

All the knights watched as Arthur put the sword back into the stone.

'Kay,' said Sir Ector. 'Draw the sword from the stone.'

So Kay put this hand around the handle of the sword and pulled. But the sword did not move. Then all the other knights tried to pull the sword out of the stone. Many strong men tried to take the sword, but it still did not move.

'Arthur,' said Sir Ector, 'draw the sword from the stone.'

Arthur put his hand on the sword and drew the sword from the stone easily. Then he raised the sword above his head and the metal flashed brightly in the sunlight. Everyone could see that Arthur held the sword.

Sir Ector got off his horse. He drew his own sword from its sheath and knelt down on the ground. He lowered his head and held the handle of his sword towards Arthur.

'Arthur,' said Ector. 'You are the true king of all the land and I am your servant.'

Arthur was astonished[20]. 'Father, put your sword away,' he said. He touched the hilt of Sir Ector's sword. Ector kissed the sword and put it back in its sheath.

The man
Who pulls this sword
from the stone is the
true king of all Britain

'Arthur,' said Ector. 'You are the true king of
all the land and I am your servant.'

'Arthur, Sire. You must know the truth,' said Sir Ector. 'I am not your father. Merlin the Magician brought you to me more than fifteen summers ago when you were only a few days old. "Take this child into your home," Merlin told me. "The boy's name is Arthur. Take care of him. Arthur and Kay will be brothers."'

Arthur is crowned King

When they heard these words, everyone knelt down. Arthur was astonished and could not speak. Then the archbishop led Arthur to the cathedral. The archbishop took the sword and laid it on the altar. Then Arthur knelt in front of the altar and prayed.

For a day and a night, Arthur prayed in the great church. He asked God to help him. He wanted to be a good and just king.

Three months passed. At the beginning of spring, Arthur was crowned king in Winchester Cathedral. When the archbishop put the crown on Arthur's head, all the people shouted, 'LONG LIVE THE KING!'

3

Excalibur

A new sword

Merlin the Magician came to Arthur. 'Sire, you will fight many battles,' he said. 'You will need a new sword.'

'But I have a sword,' Arthur replied.

'The sword that came from the stone is not for fighting,' said Merlin. 'That sword is a sign[21] that you are king. It is the Sword of Right. Now you need a sword for battle. Your new sword will be the Sword of Might. It will be a powerful, fighting sword. You must not use this sword because you are angry. You must use it to do good. You must defend the weak against the strong. You must fight against evil and defend your land.

A journey to the west

Merlin took Arthur to the lands in the west. They travelled for many days. They went through great forests and passed the dark castle at Tintagel where Arthur was born. They rode onto high, bare hills and came near to the sea.

From the top of these hills, Arthur saw a valley and a lake. In the far west, past the lake, he saw a plain of sand. Beyond the plain of sand, he saw the sea. And, on the horizon, he could see a group of islands.

Arthur and Merlin rode down the hills and into the valley until they came to the edge of the lake. There, they stood together and looked at the water. Clouds moved across the sky and the colour of the water changed from blue to green to grey. As the sun went lower in the sky, a soft, white mist came across the water. And then a boat came out of the mist.

The boat was empty, and it had no sails or oars. There was no wind, but the boat moved slowly across the water until it stopped at Arthur's feet. Then Arthur stepped inside. The boat began to move towards the middle of the lake.

The Lady of the Lake

A hand and arm rose out of the water. The arm was covered in fine white cloth. The hand held a great sword. Arthur reached out and took the sword in his own hand. As he held the sword, a voice whispered the name, 'EXCALIBUR!' Then the arm disappeared under the water.

Arthur looked at the sword. It was made of fine steel and there was writing on the blade. The words, TAKE ME UP, were written on one side of the blade. On the other side of the blade, were the words: CAST ME AWAY.

The boat moved back to the shore where Merlin was waiting.

'The sword, Excalibur, is a gift from the Lady of the Lake,' Merlin said. 'One day, you must give it back to her.'

'How shall I know that day?' asked Arthur.

'You will know that day when you come to this lake again,' Merlin answered. 'Now, it is time for battle.'

Into battle

So Arthur returned to Winchester and gathered his knights.

'We shall go to the east and to the north,' he told them. 'We shall fight the invaders who attack the coast of our land. And we shall fight against the wild men of the north.'

Then Arthur led his men to the east and fought the invaders from the sea. The villagers in the east had left their homes and were hiding in the western lands. The villages were empty.

Arthur fought six battles. He carried the sword Excalibur into each battle and defeated his enemies. The invaders ran to their ships and went back across the sea.

When the invaders had gone, the people returned to their villages. At last there was peace in the southern and eastern lands.

Next, Arthur turned to the north. There he fought six battles against the wild men of the northern lands and won a great battle at Badon Hill. After this, there was peace in the northern lands too. The northern people made Arthur their king.

Arthur had been fighting for six long years.

The Kingdom of Logres

Arthur named all his lands the Kingdom of Logres. And, at last, there was one king ruling one country. It was a time of peace and plenty[22] and the people were happy.

Camelot and the Round Table

Arthur built a castle on a hill above a river. He named the castle Camelot. Castle Camelot was made of white stone and it had many towers.

The bravest knights of Logres came to Camelot and sat with Arthur in his great hall. In the centre of the hall there was a round table which had been made by Merlin.

Many knights sat and ate and drank at this round table. Camelot became the home of King Arthur and the Knights of the Round Table.

4

Queen Guinevere

The most famous Knights

Many knights joined King Arthur at Camelot. Three of those knights – Sir Bedivere, Sir Lancelot du Lac and Sir Gawain – would always be remembered.

Sir Bedivere was the first and most faithful knight. Sir Lancelot du Lac was the bravest, the strongest and the most handsome knight. And Sir Gawain was often called the Greatest Knight because Gawain was polite and chivalrous and he did great deeds[23].

As time passed, more knights came to Camelot. They, too, did many great and good deeds. All the knights sat in special seats at the Round Table. The seats were also called 'sieges'. Each knight's name was written on their siege in letters of gold. But one seat at the table was always empty. There was no name written on it.

The Siege Perilous

'The empty seat is called the Siege Perilous,' said Merlin. 'Only one man may sit in this place. The man will be pure – a man who has never done any evil deed. I do not know his name, but the man will come to Camelot one day. Meanwhile, no other man may sit on the Siege Perilous. If they do, they will die. Then great trouble will come to Logres.'

Leodogran – the King of Cameliard

The Knights of the Round Table travelled through all the land. There were no battles to fight now, but they fought other enemies – robbers, ogres[24], and evil magicians. Arthur's knights guarded and supported their king. They also protected the poor and weak.

During this time, Arthur rode west with Sir Gawain and Merlin until they came to the land of Cameliard. The King of Cameliard was called Leodogran.

Arthur, Merlin and Gawain stopped at King Leodogran's castle. Leodogran welcomed them and took them into his hall.

'You are welcome,' he said. 'Please eat, drink and rest in my castle.'

King Leodogran was a tall man. He had a handsome and honest face and he smiled often. His daughter came into the hall and she smiled at the guests.

'This is my daughter, Guinevere,' said King Leodogran.

Guinevere was tall, and her face was very beautiful. Her hair was the colour of gold. Men said that she was the fairest and most lovely woman in the land. She came into the hall and sat on the left side of her father.

As soon as Arthur saw Guinevere, he looked at no one else. But Arthur did not behave like Uther Pendragon, his father. When Guinevere lowered her eyes, Arthur lowered his eyes too.

King Leodogran looked at them both and smiled.

Arthur spoke quietly to Merlin. 'I want to marry,' he said. 'The Kingdom of Logres must have both a king and a queen. And the kingdom must have an heir[25]. I must have a son who will be king after me. I choose Guinevere to be my Queen.'

Merlin looks into the future

Merlin looked at Arthur. The young king was tall and strong and his hair was the colour of gold. Arthur had a handsome face and clear eyes. When people looked at him, they thought of a lion. The king's voice was soft and when he spoke, men listened. Men loved Arthur because he was polite and honest and wise. They respected him because he was a great warrior and had won many battles. Arthur had brought peace to Logres.

'Merlin,' said Arthur. 'Can you look into the future? Use your magic and answer this question. Will my marriage to Guinevere bring peace and plenty to the Land of Logres?'

Merlin did not reply immediately. He looked far away towards the sea. His eyes were pale blue – the colour of the summer sky. Suddenly the colour of his eyes changed. They became dark grey – the colour of the sky during a storm.

There was sadness in Merlin's voice when he spoke. He said quietly: 'Yes, Arthur, the Land of Logres will know peace and plenty for a time. But all things must pass and all men must pass with them. Your kingdom will live in memory. Your story will last as long as men tell stories. But you shall pass away and I shall pass away and your kingdom shall pass away.'

'This is the way of the world,' said Arthur. 'I shall marry Guinevere and I shall love her and keep her. And I shall care for the land as long as I live.'

'Now I must tell you that I have looked into the future for the last time,' said Merlin. 'My powers are growing weak. My own future is dark, and, soon, I will pass away into the darkness. You will have to rule without my help. You are King Arthur and your queen shall be Guinevere. Rule the Land of Logres with justice. Make it a peaceful place.'

Arthur asks Guinevere to be his wife

Arthur went and spoke to King Leodogran. 'I wish to marry your daughter,' he said.

Leodogran looked at his daughter, Guinevere, and she smiled. 'I am happy,' said Leodogran. 'You are a great king. It will be a good marriage. And I see that my daughter is happy too.'

And so the kings made an agreement. 'I shall marry Guinevere in the spring,' Arthur said to Leodogran. 'Our wedding day will be on the holy festival which the English call Whitsun. And, before that day, I shall send my bravest knight to you. He will bring your daughter to Camelot. He will come to you in April, at the holy festival of Easter.'

'We shall wait for him at Caerleon Castle,' Leodogran said. 'Caerleon stands beside the River Usk. It is my favourite castle. I will give Caerleon Castle to you and to my daughter as a wedding gift.'

That night there was a great feast in the castle. Leodogran raised a cup and said: 'Let us drink to the health of King Arthur and Queen Guinevere.' And all the knights and people shouted: 'Long live King Arthur and Queen Guinevere!'

The Lady Nimuë

Arthur left Cameliard and rode with Merlin and Gawain to the south-west. Merlin led the way. At last, they came to a land of lakes.

'Why have we come this way?' asked Arthur.

'Someone is waiting for me here,' replied Merlin. 'I do not know who the person is, but, when I looked into the future, I saw this place.'

Nearby, they heard the sound of people fighting. Two knights were fighting beside the road. They fought with swords and shields. Two squires[26] held the knights' horses and watched the fight. A lady was standing between the two squires.

'Sirs! Why are you fighting?' Gawain called out to the knights.

'We are fighting for the lady,' one of the knights replied. 'You may not have her!'

As he said this, the knight lifted his sword and ran towards Gawain. Gawain raised his shield and drew his own sword from its sheath. The knight swung his sword and brought it down onto the neck of Gawain's warhorse, cutting off the horse's head. The horse dropped and Gawain was thrown to the ground.

'Knight!' shouted Gawain. 'Defend yourself!'

He jumped up, raised his own sword, and ran towards the knight. The knight lifted his shield, but Gawain was too strong. His sword broke the knight's shield. Then Gawain swung his sword at the knight's helmet and broke open his head. The knight fell down and died.

Then Gawain turned to the other knight, but the other did not wish to fight.

'I was defending the lady from this man, who is our enemy,' the other knight said. 'Her name is Lady Nimuë of Avalon. She is waiting for a messenger from King Arthur's court.'

Arthur and Merlin rode their horses forward. Gawain took the dead knight's horse.

'Who are you waiting for?' Arthur asked the lady.

Lady Nimuë smiled and said nothing. She looked at Merlin, and Merlin looked at Nimuë.

They said nothing, but Nimuë and Merlin spoke to each other without words. Nimuë was like Merlin. She had magical powers. She was a sorceress[27].

5

Merlin and Nimuë

Glastonbury and Morgana Le Fey

Arthur and Gawain rode along a narrow road across the watery land. Merlin followed them, carrying Nimuë on his horse. Merlin and Nimuë were always together. They used magic to speak together without words. Merlin was in love with Nimuë and he told her many secrets.

The group came to the town of Glastonbury which stands on an island in that watery land. A high hill rose behind the town and on that hill stood a small chapel. Next to it, there stood a nunnery with high walls.

Merlin and Nimuë climbed the hill. At the top they met a woman who was wearing the black clothes of a nun. Her head was covered so that no man could see her face. The woman seemed to be waiting for them.

'This lady is Morgana,' said Nimuë to Merlin. 'I have learnt magic from you. Now, Morgana will learn from you too.'

Merlin's magical powers were becoming weaker. He did not know it, but Nimuë was controlling the magician's mind. Merlin did not look at Morgana, because he only thought about Nimuë. He did not see that the nun was Morgana Le Fey – the daughter of Gorloïs and Igrayne of Cornwall. And Merlin did not remember that Morgana was Arthur's half-sister[28].

And so the two sorceresses – Nimuë and Morgana – learnt Merlin's secrets. They took more and more of the magician's power and Merlin gradually became old and weak.

The Holy Grail

Arthur and Gawain left the nunnery and went to Glastonbury Abbey[29]. Inside the abbey, there was a well of holy water. The abbess – the woman in charge of the nunnery – showed the holy well to Arthur and Gawain.

'Joseph of Arimathea[30] brought the Holy Grail to this land,' said the abbess. 'He put the Grail into this well. The water from this well can heal[31] the sick. The Grail itself can heal the land. It can stop troubles and bring peace. But the Grail was taken from us. It is not lost; it is hidden somewhere. Only the purest knight can find the Grail. He will find the Grail when there is great danger in the land.'

Merlin speaks to Arthur for the last time

Arthur, Gawain and Merlin rode back towards Camelot with Nimuë and Morgana Le Fey. Merlin spoke to Arthur.

'Sire, I shall not return to Camelot,' said the magician. 'I am going away with Nimuë and Morgana. You are king, and Guinevere is queen. You must rule without my help.'

Arthur was troubled by Merlin's words. 'Shall I never see you again?' Arthur asked.

'You will never see me in this life again,' answered Merlin. 'But we shall both return, one day. Remember, you are the Once and Future King. Now, goodbye. I shall see your wedding, and then I shall leave.'

Merlin's words made Arthur sad. But as he rode on to Camelot with Gawain, he did not think deeply about their meaning.

Lancelot becomes Champion of Camelot

Shortly before the holy week of Easter, Arthur sent for Sir Lancelot. Sir Lancelot was the strongest and most handsome the Knights of the Round Table. He always wore shining armour.

'Lancelot,' Arthur said. 'You are my bravest knight. I now make you my Champion Knight. You will guard and defend everything that I love. Ride to Caerleon Castle. My bride, Guinevere of Cameliard, is waiting there. Bring Guinevere to Camelot. She and I will be married at Whitsun. Then Guinevere will be crowned Queen.'

Lancelot smiled and bowed towards the king. 'Yes, Sire,' he said. Then he got onto his great warhorse, which was dressed in red and white cloth, and he rode away.

Lancelot meets Guinevere

Lancelot's journey to Caerleon took many days. At last he came to the castle where Guinevere was waiting.

When he met Guinevere, he saw that she was the fairest woman in the land. And Guinevere saw that Lancelot was the fairest man.

Lancelot and Guinevere rode to Camelot together, talking and laughing. Behind them rode twenty of Leodogran's finest knights. Each knight wore fine armour and fine clothes.

It was the month of May and white flowers fell from the trees onto the road. The travellers stopped and rested at a chapel where many flowers grew. Lancelot took a red rose and put it in his hair. Guinevere took a white lily and wore it on her dress.

'Lady,' said Lancelot. 'I am your servant. I shall always serve you and no other.'

The marriage of Arthur and Guinevere

They came to Camelot and saw that there were many tents in the fields. Knights had come to Camelot from many parts of Logres. Each day, the knights competed in jousts[32]. They rode their warhorses and fought with swords, shields and spears. And each evening, the knights ate, drank and told stories.

At Whitsun, Arthur married Guinevere. When he placed a crown upon her head, the knights and people gave a great cry. 'Long Live King Arthur and Queen Guinevere!' they shouted.

Morgana Le Fey plots the destruction of Camelot

That night, Merlin lay in his tent. With him were Nimuë and Morgana.

Merlin's mind was clouded and his sight was weak. He saw Morgana's smile but he did not see *behind* the smile.

Morgana hated her half-brother, Arthur, because his father, Uther Pendragon, had put Morgana in a nunnery. Because Merlin had taken Arthur away from Igrayne, Igrayne had thrown herself into the sea. Morgana hated Merlin as well.

While Merlin slept, Morgana cast two spells. The first spell was for Guinevere. It made Guinevere sleep in her own bedchamber and dream of Lancelot. With the second spell, she made herself look like Guinevere. Then she went to Arthur's bedchamber where Arthur was sleeping. He was dreaming of battle and wounds. He dreamt that he lost his sword, Excalibur. He dreamt that nothing grew on the land. Then Morgana came to Arthur's bed and lay with him.

As the sorceress lay with the king, bright lightning flashed in the sky. And when Morgana left Arthur, she whispered to her half-brother. 'I will have a son,' she said. 'He will be like your father, Uther Pendragon. Sleep well, brother.' And Arthur slept and forgot his dreams.

And so Morgana brought evil and sadness to the court of Camelot. Though, many long years passed before anyone knew that this had happened.

The passing of Merlin

Early the next morning, Merlin left his tent. He had become an old man. He was so ill and weak that Nimuë and Morgana had to help him onto his horse. Then they led the magician away from Camelot, towards the north.

'Merlin, I know a place where you will be young again,' said Nimuë. 'It is a secret place in a forest. We will take you there and you can rest.'

'Yes, yes,' said Merlin. But he did not see who spoke to him, or what was near him. He did not see the trees of the great forest around him. He did not see how they had come to a secret place in the forest where a circle of tall stones stood around a low hill. On the top of the hill, there was a great oak tree. Nimuë and Morgana led Merlin to the tree. Then, a doorway opened in the trunk of the tree. A light was burning inside.

'Step inside the tree, Merlin,' said Nimuë. 'Here you will find rest. You are old and tired. Soon you will feel young again. Here you may sleep through many centuries and dream of the world outside. Rest here – until the day when you shall wake and return to the land again.'

Merlin stepped into the oak tree and the door closed behind him. There, inside the oak, he slept and dreamed of the world outside.

'No man shall see his face again,' said Morgana to Nimuë.

From that day, no one saw Merlin the Magician again. But the people often spoke his name and told their children stories about him.

6

Sir Gawain and the Green Knight

Christmas court

It was a time of peace in the Kingdom of Logres. King Arthur and Queen Guinevere ruled wisely and well. Many good and noble[33] knights visited Camelot and the Round Table. Many stories were told of famous knights there – of Lancelot, Gawain, Tristram, Percivale and Galahad. And their stories are still told today.

Every year, on Christmas Day, King Arthur gathered the knights at his court in Camelot. Everyone celebrated for twelve days. There was a great feast. Everyone ate good food and drank wine. They danced and listened to stories.

Then, one year, on the twelfth day of Christmas, a strange knight rode into the court. He was the strangest knight that anyone had seen. He was tall and broad, like the trunk of a tree. His great warhorse had fierce, red eyes. The knight was not wearing armour, but he and his horse were both dressed in green cloth.

Even more strangely, both the knight and his horse were green. The skin of the horse was green and the skin of the knight was green. The knight's hair and beard were green too. The Green Knight did not carry a sword. He held a huge green and gold axe in his right hand.

The knight rode his horse through the gates of Camelot Castle. He rode into the great hall and stopped in front of the Round Table. Here, the best knights sat in the most important seats. Only one seat still remained empty at the table. This was the Siege Perilous.

The Green Knight looked around the hall. 'Where is the

king of this land?' he asked in a loud voice. 'I will speak with the king and no other man.'

The guests at the feast were astonished. No one had ever seen such a knight. He was the colour of new grass and leaves in spring. And he had ridden his horse into the hall!

'Sir knight, you are welcome,' said Arthur. 'Will you join us at the feast?'

'I do not come to eat and drink,' said the Green Knight. 'I come to see the brave and famous knights at your court.'

'Sir, there are many good knights here,' said Arthur. 'And many of them are ready to fight and to joust.'

The Green Knight challenges[34] the knights of Camelot

'I come from my castle in the north,' said the Green Knight. 'I make this challenge. Who will strike me with my own axe? Is any knight brave enough?'

He held the heavy green axe above his head. The knights of Camelot looked at it and were silent.

'Come, any man,' said the Green Knight. 'Take my axe. You may strike the first blow. You may cut off my head. I will strike the second blow. That is my only request.'

No one spoke. The Green Knight laughed. 'Are there no brave knights here? Do you all fear me? I speak truthfully. You may strike the first blow and I shall strike the second.'

'If no man will take your challenge,' said Arthur, 'I shall strike the blow myself. But you do not bring honour to my court. Your challenge is not honourable. Go in peace and do not return. This is a feast day, not a day of battle.'

Sir Gawain takes the challenge

The Green Knight laughed again. 'You fear that you cannot kill me with one blow from my axe,' he shouted. 'You fear that I will kill you. Is this what you brave men of Camelot think?'

'Who will strike me with my own axe?'

Then Gawain stood up. 'I am Gawain, son of King Lot,' he said. 'I will strike you with your axe. I will cut off your head.'

'Do it,' said the Green Knight. 'Then, after this day, twelve months and one day will pass. At that time, you shall come to my castle in the north. There I shall strike you with my axe and I will cut off your head. This will be our bargain[35].'

'Give me the axe,' said Gawain. 'I accept your bargain. But I will strike only once and you will never strike your own stroke. Go in peace, or you will die today.'

The Green Knight laughed. He got down from his horse and gave his axe to Gawain. Then he knelt down on the floor. 'Strike my neck, knight,' he said. 'Strike well. Remember our bargain.'

Sir Gawain took the green axe. It was a heavy axe and Gawain held it in both hands. 'I am a Knight of the Round Table,' he said. 'I do not break my word; but I give you a last chance to change your mind and leave in peace.'

'Strike!' shouted the Green Knight. 'What are you waiting for? Are you afraid? Strike me with my axe and cut off my head.'

Gawain raised the axe in both hands and struck the Green Knight's neck. The Green Knight's head rolled onto the floor.

The Green Knight is not dead

Then the knights and ladies of Camelot watched with astonishment. The Green Knight stood up. Then he picked up his head and held it by the hair. The eyes in the head looked at Gawain and the mouth moved and it spoke these words: 'I am the Knight of the Green Chapel in the north. You will come to the Green Chapel in one year and one day. Then I will cut off your head.'

Then, holding his head in his hand, the Green Knight got onto his horse. He rode out of the hall and out of Castle Camelot.

Everyone was silent. The feast was ended. 'Gawain has made a terrible bargain,' thought the Knights of the Round Table. 'He has just agreed to his own death.'

Sir Gawain journeys north

The year passed quickly. On the first day of the twelfth month, Arthur and his courtiers were at Caerleon. The knights said goodbye to Gawain.

Gawain put on his armour and his sword. He got onto his warhorse. A squire gave Gawain his shield. 'I will begin my quest,' said Gawain. 'I will go and look for the Green Chapel. I do this for the honour of Camelot and the glory of Logres.'

Gawain's journey was long and dangerous. He rode north into the forests where dark creatures lived. He did battle with robbers and ogres. He crossed rocky hills of stone and snow and cold streams where the ice broke. It was deep midwinter and colder than any man could remember. He stopped at every village and asked where he could find the Green Chapel.

At last, Gawain came to a deep valley. A wide stream ran in the bottom of this valley. On the other side of the stream, there was no snow on the ground. Here, the grass was green.

On the other side of the valley, there was a castle on a hill. Gawain went into the valley and rode through the stream. Then he went up to the castle and knocked on the gate.

'I am Gawain, from the court of King Arthur!' he shouted. 'I am seeking the Green Chapel.'

A servant opened the castle gate. 'My lord says that you are welcome,' said the man. 'Please come into the castle and rest.'

Gawain went into the castle. The servant took his horse to the stables. Then he led Gawain into the castle hall.

The lord of the castle was a tall man who had a thin, pale face. 'Welcome, Sir Gawain,' said the lord. 'It is Christmas – a time of peace and celebration. Will you stay with us and rest?'

Gawain sat by the warm fire. 'I thank you, sir,' he said. Then he ate the good food that the lord of the castle gave him.

'I seek the Green Chapel and the Green Knight,' said Gawain, when he had finished eating.

'The Green Chapel is near here,' replied the lord. 'You will find it at the end of this valley. But the Green Knight is a cruel man. Do not seek him. He will kill you.'

'I have made a bargain with the Green Knight,' replied Gawain. 'And I must keep this promise. I am a Knight of the Round Table. I cannot break my promise.'

'Very well,' said the lord of the castle. 'Rest here and you will find the Green Chapel tomorrow.'

The lady of the castle gives Gawain a green ribbon

The lady of the castle took Gawain to a bedchamber. The room was warm and the bed was soft. The lady brought hot wine to Gawain and smiled. She spoke softly and laughed easily. Gawain saw that she was very beautiful.

'You are a handsome knight,' said the lady. 'It is a cold night. Would you like a maiden[36] of the castle to visit you?'

'No, lady,' said Gawain. 'I thank you for the food and the fire. But I am on a quest. I will not bring honour to you or your lord if I spend time with your maidens.'

'You are a good and honorable knight,' said the lady. 'I have a gift for you. It is a small thing – a piece of green ribbon[37]. The ribbon will protect you. You must wear it in your hair.'

So Gawain tied the green ribbon in his hair. Then he slept.

The Green Chapel

Early the next morning, Gawain rode out of the castle and rode along the valley until he saw the Green Chapel. Outside the chapel sat the Green Knight. His head was back on his shoulders and his green face was angry.

The Green Knight was sharpening the blade of his axe.

'You have come a long way, Sir Gawain,' said the Green Knight. 'I am surprised. You have made a long journey to die.'

'I am here because I made you a promise,' answered Sir Gawain. 'I am a Knight of the Round Table at Camelot and I do not break my promises.'

'Very well,' said the Green Knight. 'Then you must prepare to die.'

Sir Gawain watched and waited as the Green Knight came close and swung his axe. Gawain heard the sound of the blade as it went through the air. But Gawain's head did not fall from his neck. Something else fell to the ground. It was the green ribbon – the gift from the lady of the castle.

Sir Gawain keeps his promise

Suddenly the face of the Green Knight changed. His skin was no longer green. His hair and beard were no longer green. Instead he became a tall man with a pale, thin face. He was the lord of the castle where Gawain had rested. Then his lady came out of the Green Chapel and stood beside her lord. She smiled at Gawain.

'The green ribbon was a sign to my husband,' she said. 'It is a sign that you are a man of honour.'

'Sir Gawain, you have proved that you are a good and honorable knight,' said the lord of the castle. 'Now you must return to Camelot and tell this story. From this day forward, men will say: "Sir Gawain did not break his promise to the Green Knight."'

7

The Chapel Perilous

Sir Lancelot seeks adventure

Sir Lancelot du Lac rode out of Camelot in search of adventure. He rode for many days until he found a forest full of tall trees that hid the sun. There were many paths through the trees, but Lancelot did not know which one to take.

Suddenly a white hunting dog came out of the trees. The dog put its nose to the ground and ran along one of the paths.

'Perhaps the dog will lead me to its master,' thought Lancelot. So Lancelot followed the dog along the path.

Lancelot looked at the ground and saw that there was a trail of blood on the path. The dog was following the trail of blood and Lancelot followed the dog. The dog kept turning its head to look at Lancelot.

The dog led Lancelot out of the forest. They went over a bridge to a large house. When the dog ran into the house, Lancelot got off his horse. He went into the house and saw a knight lying on the floor of the hall. The knight was wearing black armour. Blood ran from many wounds on the knight's body. He was dead.

Lancelot heard a sound outside the house. He went outside and saw a lady in the garden. Her hands were covering her eyes and she was crying.

The curse of Lady Gilbert

'What has happened?' Lancelot asked. The lady took her hands from her face and raised her head. Lancelot saw that she had an ugly red mark on her face.

'Sir Meliot came here,' answered the lady. 'He fought my husband and killed him. But Sir Meliot was wounded in the fight. The wound will never heal and Sir Meliot will die.'

'I know Sir Meliot,' said Lancelot. 'He is a Knight of the Round Table at Camelot. He is a good and honorable knight.'

The lady looked angrily at Lancelot. 'Go back to Camelot!' she cried. 'I am Lady Gilbert. My husband, Sir Gilbert, is the dead knight. I can make magic. I have cursed Sir Meliot. Now his wound will never heal. Go! ... or I will curse you too!'

Lancelot quickly left the house. The white hunting dog was waiting for him outside. The dog barked and ran along a path. Lancelot got onto his horse and followed. He rode back into the dark forest.

Soon they came to another large house. Another lady was sitting in the garden. She too, was crying, but as soon as she saw Lancelot she dried her eyes. The dog went to the lady and licked her hand.

Sir Meliot has a wound that will not heal

'I know you,' said the lady, 'You are Sir Lancelot du Lac. You know my brother, Sir Meliot.'

'Did Sir Meliot fight with Sir Gilbert today?' asked Lancelot.

'Yes, he did,' answered Sir Meliot's sister. 'Lady Gilbert is an evil sorceress. She has used magic. She has put a curse on Sir Meliot. He is wounded and his wound will not heal.'

Lancelot went into the house and found Sir Meliot lying in the hall. The knight had a bleeding wound on the left side of his body.

'Only a cloth from Chapel Perilous will heal my brother,' said Sir Meliot's sister. 'That is what Lady Gilbert told me.'

'Then I will go to Chapel Perilous and find this cloth,' said Lancelot.

'No man has gone into Chapel Perilous and returned alive,' said the lady. 'The chapel is in the middle of the forest. The knights who guard it are really dead but they still seem alive. They are controlled by Lady Gilbert's magic powers.'

'I do not fear any knights – living or dead,' said Lancelot.

'Then follow this path,' said the lady. She pointed to a path through the forest. 'The path is too narrow for your horse. You must walk. But Chapel Perilous is not far. Take my dog. The dog will guide you.'

Lancelot walked along the path until he came to the middle of the forest. Here, he saw a small chapel that was made of dark stones. The shields of many knights were hanging on a tree outside the chapel. These shields were upside down, which was a sign that the knights were dead.

The dead knights

The knights were standing near their shields. They did not move. Their armour was old and dark and they held swords in their hands. Lancelot stepped closer to them.

The knights turned slowly and looked at Lancelot. He saw their faces and knew that the knights were dead men. These were the knights who had entered Chapel Perilous. The knights opened their mouths but they could not speak. They looked at Lancelot with empty eyes.

Lancelot drew his sword and ran towards the knights. He swung his sword, but it passed straight through the bodies of the knights. And the knights could not strike Lancelot with their swords. The knights who guarded the chapel were ghosts.

Sir Lancelot enters the Chapel Perilous

So Sir Lancelot entered the Chapel Perilous. There were no windows in the walls, but many lamps hung from the ceiling.

Strange shadows moved on the walls. At the end of the chapel, there was a large, flat stone. The body of a knight was lying on this stone. Lancelot went to the body and saw that it was covered with a silk cloth. He cut a piece of the cloth with his sword and held it in his hand.

Suddenly, there was a sound like thunder. Then the floor moved. Lancelot walked back to the doorway and went outside. The dead knights stood in front of Lancelot and he could not pass. The ghosts did not move their mouths, but Lancelot heard their terrible voices.

'Knight! Do not take the cloth from the chapel,' they said. 'If you take the cloth, you will die. And you will never see Guinevere again.'

'Ghosts! You have no power over me,' said Lancelot. 'Let me pass.'

Lancelot swung his sword at the dead knights. But he could not fight them. The knights did not have bodies like living men. Instead, they pushed against Sir Lancelot like the thick smoke of a fire.

Lancelot swung his sword, but he could not fight smoke. Then, looking up into the light, Lancelot saw the shields that hung on chains above the entrance to the chapel. Lancelot cut at the chains and the shields began to fall. As one by one, each shield fell, one by one, a dead knight fell to the ground. When Lancelot had cut down all the shields, all the knights had fallen. Then Lancelot heard a great cry. The Lady Gilbert was standing at the entrance to the Chapel Perilous. She put her hand to the red mark on her face and then she too sank to the ground.

Sir Lancelot takes the cloth to Sir Meliot

Lancelot walked back to the house of Sir Meliot. The sun was bright and birds sang. Lancelot gave the cloth from Chapel

Perilous to Sir Meliot's sister. She smiled. 'Thank you,' she said. Then she led Lancelot to her brother.

'The Lady Gilbert is dead,' said Sir Lancelot. 'I have brought a cloth from the Chapel Perilous to heal your wound.'

Sir Meliot's skin was pale and he was near to death. Blood flowed from the wound in his side but as soon as the cloth touched his wound, the blood stopped flowing. Then Sir Meliot opened his eyes.

'I am healed,' he said. 'Lady Gilbert was an evil sorceress whose real name was Hellawes. She was a companion[38] of Morgana Le Fey. The power of Hellawes is broken now. But she cast a spell on another lady who lives near this forest. And that spell may not be broken.'

'I will return to Camelot,' said Lancelot. 'And I will tell the story of Hellawes the Sorceress and Chapel Perilous.'

Sir Meliot and his sister thanked Lancelot.

'Farewell,' said Lancelot. 'Sir Meliot, we will meet again, at the Round Table in Camelot.'

The Fair Maid of Astolat

Lancelot rode through forests until he came to a river that runs down to Camelot. A tall grey tower stood on an island in the river. The island was called the Isle of Astolat. Elaine, the Fair Maid of Astolat, lived in the tall tower.

No man had seen Elaine. She lived in the highest room of the tower. The room's walls had no windows, but it was bright because light came through windows in the ceiling. There were many mirrors on the walls that reflected this light. Elaine looked at the mirrors and she saw the world outside her tower.

The tower of mirrors

Years before, when the sorceress Hellawes gained her evil powers, her face had been spoilt with an ugly red mark. After that, Hellawes hated all beautiful women.

'No man wishes to see my face,' she said. 'But all men wish to see the face of the Fair Maid of Astolat. So I will put a curse on her. If Elaine looks at any man, she will die.'

Elaine knew that she could not look at the world outside her tower. And, so, she watched the world with her mirrors and she used coloured silk threads to make a tapestry[39]. The tapestry showed pictures of the world.

When Sir Lancelot came riding out of the forest, the sunlight flashed on the knight's bright armour. Elaine saw the bright flash in her mirror. She watched the knight as he rode closer to her tower. Lancelot was not wearing a helmet, so Elaine saw his face clearly.

Elaine had seen men reflected in her mirror, but she had never met a man. And she had never seen a man as handsome as Lancelot. She did not want the reflection of Lancelot to disappear from her mirror.

Forgetting the curse, Elaine ran from her room to the top of the tower. She opened the door and looked down at the knight's handsome face. But Lancelot did not see Elaine.

The curse

Suddenly the room at the top of the tower became dark. Sunlight no longer shone onto the mirrors and at once there was a great noise. The mirrors had broken and the floor was covered with broken glass.

Elaine fell to the floor. 'The curse has come to Astolat!' she cried.

Then she slowly walked down the stairs of her tower and went outside into the sunlight for the first and last time in her life. She walked to the river.

Sir Lancelot rode on towards Camelot. He heard and saw none of these things on the Isle of Astolat. He thought only of Camelot. Castle Camelot was near and he wanted to see Guinevere again. He thought of telling stories at the Round Table.

The death of Elaine

That day, there was a feast in Camelot. All the courtiers, knights and ladies ate and drank in the great hall. King Arthur and Queen Guinevere listened to stories of Sir Lancelot's adventures. But, in the middle of the feast, there was a sudden storm outside. The knights, ladies and courtiers went silent and the musicians stopped playing their music. And in the silence, they heard someone singing a sad song. The music came from outside the castle, from the direction of the river.

Everyone went to the windows and looked out from the towers of Camelot. They saw a boat floating along the river. In the boat sat a fair maiden who was singing the sad song. Before the boat reached Camelot, the maiden lay down and died.

All the people left the castle and went down to the river. The boat was dressed with brightly-coloured cloth and the maiden lay on soft, silk cushions. Her body was covered with a long tapestry with pictures made from coloured silk threads. The words, THE MAID OF ASTOLAT, were written on the boat.

Lancelot looked at the dead maiden. 'She has a beautiful face,' he said.

8

Tristram and Iseult

A minstrel[40] comes to Camelot

King Arthur sat at the Round Table and Lancelot and Gawain sat opposite him. But the seat between Lancelot and Gawain, the Siege Perilous, was still empty.

'No man has ever sat in the Siege Perilous,' said Arthur. 'Merlin told us many years ago that only the purest knight would sit in this place. But who will that knight be?'

'Perhaps it will be a knight who has not yet come to Camelot,' said Gawain.

'Sire,' said Lancelot. 'A minstrel has come to Camelot who plays a harp[41] and tells stories. He has travelled to Ireland and knows many stories. Perhaps he can tell us the name of a famous knight whom we do not know.'

So Arthur called the minstrel to the great hall. All the knights and their ladies sat and waited for the minstrel to tell a story.

The minstrel was tall and he had a fair face. But his clothes were poor and his shoes were old. He held a harp in his hand. He touched the strings of the harp with his fingers and it made a sweet sound.

The story of Tristram

'I will tell the story of Tristram,' the minstrel said in a clear voice. 'Tristram is a knight of Lyonesse – a land in the far west. King Mark of Cornwall is Sir Tristram's uncle.

'Before Arthur became king, there was war between Cornwall and Ireland. The rulers of Ireland were King Gurman and Queen Isaud. The armies of Cornwall and Ireland fought each other and Cornwall was defeated.

'Isaud's brother, Marhault, was a fierce warrior. He was the King of Ireland's champion. Marhault had black hair, cruel eyes and strong hands. He left Ireland and went to Cornwall. He spoke to King Mark.

'"The people and the land of Cornwall belong to King Gurman of Ireland now," said Marhault. "You must send a gift to Ireland. You must send fifteen boys and fifteen girls to be servants in Ireland."'

The gift

'But King Mark replied: "No! I will not send this gift."

'"Then tell your champion to fight me," said Marhault to Mark. "I am the Champion of King Gurman of Ireland and I can kill any man here. You must either fight me or send the gift to Ireland."

'At first no knight stepped forward to fight Marhault. But then a young man named Tristram stood up. "I will fight Marhault and bring honour to my king," he said.

'So Marhault laughed and drew his sword. "It will take only a moment to kill this boy," he said.

'Tristram drew his sword too. The two men fought a long and hard fight. After a time, Marhault struck a terrible blow to Tristram's leg. Then Tristram struck a blow to Marhault's head. Both men were badly wounded.

'Marhault fell to the ground. "My sword is poisoned!" he shouted to Tristram. "Your wound will not heal. You will die."'

The minstrel was silent for a moment. Everyone in the hall of Camelot was enjoying this story.

'Please continue,' said King Arthur.

The minstrel bowed to the king and continued his story.

Tristram's wound

'So Marhault's men carried their master to his ship and they sailed to Ireland. Marhault's sister, Queen Isaud, was a skilful healer. But Marhault's wounds were very bad and even Queen Isaud could not save him. And soon he died.

'Meanwhile, Tristram lay in the castle at Tintagel. No one could heal his wound.

'"Queen Isaud of Ireland is the most powerful healer in the world," said the wise men of King Mark's court. "Only Queen Isaud can heal this young man's wound. But Isaud is the enemy of Cornwall."'

When they heard this, some of the ladies of King Arthur's court began to cry.

The minstrel held up his hand. 'My story has not ended,' he said.

King Gurman and Queen Isaud

'Tristram went to Ireland. He could not walk because of the wound on his leg. Two servants carried him to the court of King Gurman. Tristram wore the clothes of a minstrel and he sang songs. Tristram sang so well that King Gurman asked him to sing in the hall of his castle.

'"How did you receive your wound?" asked King Gurman.

'"I was travelling on a ship to Ireland," Tristram replied. "Pirates[42] attacked the ship and I was wounded. The pirates killed all the other men on the ship, but they did not kill me. The pirates let me live because I played the harp and sang so well."

'Queen Isaud believed Tristram's story. "I will heal your wound," she said. And she took the minstrel to a room where he stayed for many days. Queen Isaud cared for him and healed his wound.

'After he became well, Tristram stayed in Ireland. He played the harp and sang at the court.'

Iseult the Fair

'Gurman and Isaud had one child – a daughter. The girl's name was Iseult and all men called her Iseult the Fair.

'King Gurman asked Tristram to teach his daughter. "I want Iseult to sing and to play the harp," said the king. "Please be her teacher."

'So Tristram stayed in Ireland and taught Iseult. Tristram quickly began to love Iseult, but he told no one of his feelings.

'After a time, Tristram left Ireland and returned to Cornwall. He told King Mark what had happened in the court of King Gurman and Queen Isaud. Then a wise man spoke to King Mark.

'"Sire, there is a way to end the war between Cornwall and Ireland," he said. "If you marry Iseult the Fair, there will be peace."

'King Mark thought carefully. "I have heard of Iseult the Fair," he said. "All men speak of her beauty. I will marry her and bring peace to Cornwall and Ireland. But will Gurman and Isaud agree?"'

The minstrel paused a moment. His face was sad. Then he continued his story.

The Dragon[43] of Ireland

'At that time, there was a dragon that lived in Ireland. This huge, terrible creature breathed fire from its mouth. It used that fire to destroy many villages. It killed hundreds of men, women and children.

'"Whoever kills the dragon can marry my daughter," King Gurman told his knights. "And he shall have half of my kingdom as a wedding gift."

'Tristram heard King Gurman's promise. He put on his sword and his armour, and he returned to Ireland. He did not go to the court of King Gurman and Queen Isaud. He went straight to the place where the dragon lived.

'The dragon's home was a cave, which was inside a hill. The entrance of the cave was surrounded by black rocks. The rocks were black because flames had come from the dragon's mouth and burned them. Many knights had tried to kill the dragon, but they had failed. Their bones lay on the ground outside the cave.

'Tristram watched the cave from the top of a hill. He saw three knights riding towards the cave. They carried swords and shields and spears.

'Then smoke and flames came from the cave. Tristram heard the cries of men and the sounds of fighting.

'Tristram got on his horse and rode towards the cave. The dragon was standing by the bodies of the dead knights. The dragon's back was covered in hard, green and blue skin. It had long, sharp claws[44] on its feet. Its teeth were sharp and white and smoke came from its mouth.

'Tristram lifted his spear and rode his horse straight towards the dragon. The dragon opened its mouth to burn the knight. Tristram's spear went into the dragon's mouth and down its throat.

'The dragon roared loudly. Then it struck its claws into the body of Tristram's horse and killed it. Tristram was thrown to the ground, but he got up quickly.

'The dragon was badly wounded. Tristram's spear was in its throat. When the dragon finally fell to the ground, Tristram ran towards it. He drove his sword into the dragon's soft stomach and killed it.'

The Knights of the Round Table were enjoying this story. They laughed and smiled.

Tristram claims Iseult for King Mark

The minstrel held up his hand and continued his story.

'Tristram cut off the dragon's head and took it to King Gurman. "You have been to this court before," said Queen Isaud. "You are a minstrel. You taught my daughter to play the harp. Are you also a knight?"

'Tristram answered in a clear voice. "Yes," he replied. He turned towards King Gurman. "I am Sir Tristram of Lyonesse," he said. "I am the Champion of King Mark of Cornwall. I have killed the dragon. Now King Mark can marry your daughter. My king no longer wants to make war against Ireland. He wants peace between our two countries."

'King Gurman turned and spoke to Queen Isaud. "Sir Tristram is a good and honest knight," he said. "The marriage between King Mark and our daughter will bring honour to both our countries."

'"Prepare my ship," said King Gurman. "Sir Tristram will take our daughter Iseult to Cornwall. There, she will marry King Mark."

'That night, Queen Isaud spoke secretly to her daughter's servant. "I have made a love potion[45]," she told him. "The potion is in this bottle of wine. You must take the bottle to Cornwall. There, King Mark and my daughter Iseult must drink the wine on their wedding day. It will make them love each other forever. Do not let anyone else drink the wine."

'Then Tristram and Iseult left Ireland. The wind was fresh. The ship sailed swiftly like a white bird. Tristram and Iseult talked and laughed in the spring sunlight. Tristram was sailing home. Soon Iseult began to fall in love with the young knight.'

The love potion

'Iseult's servant did not like the sea. She felt ill, so she lay down and slept. And while she slept, Tristram saw the bottle of wine. "Let us drink and be happy," he said to Iseult.

'Tristram and Iseult drank the love potion. Already they loved one another and the potion made their love stronger. Now they loved one another until the ending of the world, and they loved with a love greater than any in the world.

'The ship reached Cornwall and King Mark welcomed Tristram. "You are my greatest knight and my champion," said King Mark. "And Iseult is the fairest maiden in the world. We shall be married immediately."

'So, King Mark married Iseult the Fair. But Iseult loved Tristram and after her wedding to King Mark, Queen Iseult met Sir Tristram in secret. They met in forests and places where no one saw them. But people soon began to talk about Iseult the Fair and the king's champion. The other knights spoke to King Mark. "Your wife and the Champion are untrue to you. They are lovers," said the knights.'

Tristram and Iseult are parted

'When King Mark heard this news, he was angry. "If this is true, then Tristram must die," he said. "And Iseult shall live in a nunnery so that no man may see her face again."

'But King Mark was not a cruel man. He loved Iseult and remembered the brave deeds of his champion, Sir Tristram.

'King Mark spoke to Tristram: "Leave my kingdom and never return," he said. "You will never see Iseult the Fair again."'

Here, the minstrel ended his story.

No one spoke in the great hall of Camelot. There was only one sound – the sound of someone crying. Tears were falling from Lancelot's eyes.

'Minstrel, how do you know this sad story?' asked King Arthur. 'And is it a true story?'

'Yes, Sire,' answered the minstrel. 'I know that the story is true because I am Tristram of Lyonesse.'

'Welcome, Sir Tristram of Lyonesse,' said Arthur. 'There is a seat for you here at the Round Table.'

Sir Tristram becomes a Knight of the Round Table

So, Tristram stayed in Camelot and became a Knight of the Round Table. He did many good deeds and lived happily in Camelot. But he never forgot Iseult the Fair and he wanted to see her again.

Tristram married, several years later. His wife's name was also Iseult – but she was called Iseult of the White Hands. Tristram was a kind and good husband, but he did not love his wife. Sir Tristram loved Iseult the Fair. His wife, Iseult of the White Hands, knew this and she was jealous. Even after King Mark died, Tristram of Lyonesse could not be with Iseult the Fair because he was married to Iseult of the White Hands.

Tristram sends for Iseult

One day, a man attacked Tristram while he was riding in Lyonesse. Tristram fought the man and killed him. But the man had a poisoned spear which wounded Tristram in the thigh.

'I am going to die,' Tristram said to his servant, Kurwenal. 'There is poison in the wound, and it cannot heal. Only Iseult the Fair can save me. She is a great healer, like her mother. Take a ship to Tintagel and fetch the Fair Iseult.'

Then Tristram spoke to Kurwenal again. 'I may die before Fair Iseult arrives,' he said. 'Or she may not come at all. So, I beg you, make me this promise: if Iseult the Fair comes, raise a white sail on your ship. If she will not come, raise a black sail.

If I see a white sail, I will live until Fair Iseult comes to heal me.'

Iseult of the White Hands heard these words and there was jealousy in her heart as she watched Kurwenal leave for Tintagel. But she looked after her husband and did not speak of her feelings.

The black sail and the white sail

Kurwenal sailed to Tintagel and spoke to Queen Iseult the Fair. 'Sir Tristram is wounded,' he said. 'He will die unless you help him. He asks you to come with me to Lyonesse.'

So Iseult the Fair left Tintagel to help Tristram. She sailed with Kurwenal towards Lyonesse.

Kurwenal remembered his promise to Tristram. He raised a white sail on the ship.

At last, they came near to Sir Tristram's castle on the coast. Tristram was very ill. He could not rise from his bed. He was dying.

'Is Kurwenal returning? Is his ship near?' he asked his wife, Iseult of the White Hands. 'Do you see the sail? What colour is the sail?'

Iseult of the White Hands looked out of the window. She saw a ship with a white sail on the sea. But there was jealousy in her heart. 'I see a black sail,' she said.

The death of Tristram and Iseult

Then Tristram's great heart broke. 'I will never see Iseult the Fair again!' he said softly. He turned his face from the window and died.

And when Iseult the Fair came to Tristram, she found that he was dead. She knelt beside her lover and wept. But Tristram and Iseult could not be parted by death. Their love was so strong that Iseult the Fair lay down and died beside the noble Tristram.

Tristram and Iseult were buried[46] together in one grave[47]. Iseult of the White Hands planted two rose bushes on their grave. One bush was of red roses and the other bush was of white roses. And the two bushes grew together and became one.

9

Percivale and Lancelot

Percivale goes to Caerleon

Percivale grew up in the land west of Caerleon. It was a wild and empty land and few travellers went there. Percivale looked after his family's goats.

One day, Sir Lancelot rode through the wild land and saw Percivale. Percivale was a tall and strong young man with fair hair. He was looking after goats near the roadway.

'You are a fine young man,' said Lancelot lightly. 'You will make a good squire at the king's court. Go to Caerleon and say that Sir Lancelot sent you.'

Lancelot spoke lightly, but Percivale listened seriously. 'I will go to the king's court at Caerleon and see these knights,' Percivale told his mother. 'I do not want to look after goats all my life.'

His mother said, 'You are young and innocent. You do not know the ways of the world. Do not go to Caerleon.'

But Percivale went to Caerleon to see the king's court. He walked into the castle where the knights were feasting and he saw King Arthur.

The Red Knight

Arthur was talking to Sir Kay. He was holding a golden cup in his hand. It was the cup from which all knights drank at the Round Table.

Suddenly, a strange knight came into the hall. The knight was wearing red armour.

'Give me that cup,' said the Red Knight. 'I will drink to the best knight here.' Then he took the cup from Sir Kay's hand, left the hall and rode away.

'Who will fetch my gold cup from the Red Knight?' asked Arthur.

'I will go!' shouted all the knights at once.

'This Red Knight is unworthy[48] of a Knight of the Round Table,' Arthur said. 'Send a squire to fetch my cup.'

Then Percivale stepped forward. He was wearing the simple clothes of a goat-herd. 'I will fetch your cup,' he said.

Sir Kay laughed. 'What can a goat-herd do against a knight?'

'I want to be a knight,' said Percivale.

Sir Kay laughed again, but Arthur spoke gently. 'Young man,' he said, 'you have an honest face. If you can bring me the gold cup, I will make you a knight. Now, you may take a horse and follow the Red Knight.'

Percivale mounted a horse and rode after the Red Knight. Arthur spoke to Sir Gawain and Sir Gareth. 'Ride after him. Look after him and make sure that he comes to no harm.' And so Gawain and Gareth rode after the young Percivale.

Percivale rode quickly and soon found the Red Knight. 'That gold cup is not yours,' he called out.

The Red Knight stopped his horse and turned to Percivale. 'What can a young boy like you do against a knight?' he asked.

'I will fight you,' said Percivale, 'because you are an unworthy and untrue knight.'

'Then I will have to kill you,' said the Red Knight. He pointed his lance and rode at Percivale. But Percivale was quick. He jumped from his horse and pulled the Red Knight's spear from his hand. Then the Red Knight turned and drew his sword. But Percivale ran at the knight and drove the spear into the knight's throat. The Red Knight fell from his horse and Percivale picked up the golden cup.

Sir Gawain and Sir Gareth saw the cup in Percivale's hand, and they saw the dead knight on the ground. They took Percivale back to Caerleon and spoke to the king.

'This young man killed the Red Knight and took the cup,' they told him. 'He is brave enough and worthy enough to be a knight.'

So Percivale became a knight. Sir Lancelot taught Percivale to use a sword and they rode to Camelot together.

Naciens the hermit[49]

Then, at Easter time, a holy hermit called Naciens came to Camelot. 'I come to ask for help,' he said to King Arthur. 'I know a lady who is imprisoned in a tower. Only a brave and pure knight can save her. She is being kept prisoner by an evil sorceress.'

'Sire,' Lancelot said, 'I will rescue the lady. And I will take Sir Percivale with me.'

'I thank you,' said the hermit and looked at the Round Table. 'I see there is an empty seat. Who sits there?'

'No man sits in the Siege Perilous,' Arthur answered. 'Many years ago, Merlin said that only the purest, most worthy knight would one day come to sit there.'

Naciens the hermit looked at the Siege Perilous and nodded his head. Then he led Sir Lancelot and Sir Percivale out of Camelot. After a long journey, they came to a dark hillside with a black tower on the top of the hill.

'That is the Dolorous Tower,' said the hermit. 'The lady is a prisoner in that tower.'

The Dolorous Tower

So Lancelot and Percivale rode up to the tower. The door was made of wood and was fastened with an iron lock. Lancelot and Percivale struck the iron lock with their swords and the door opened.

When they broke the door, they also broke the spell that kept the lady prisoner. The lady of the tower spoke to the knights and said, 'I am the Lady Blanchefleur. I was a prisoner of Queen Morgana Le Fey. She is an enemy of my father. Now, will you come to my father so that he may thank you. My father lives in Castle Carbonek.'

King Pelles

The knights and Lady Blanchefleur rode across a waste land to an old castle. Here, two squires met them and took their horses. Then the squires led the knights into the castle hall.

An old king lay on a bed in the hall. 'I am King Pelles,' he said. 'Years ago I was wounded in the thigh. That wound will not heal. I cannot rise from this bed. I thank you for rescuing my daughter. I ask you to stay here and rest.'

The first vision[50] of the Holy Grail

So Lancelot and Percivale rested in the castle. They ate in the great hall. And while they were eating, they heard the sound of music. A bright light shone from high above. Then three women came into the hall. They were dressed in white and their faces were covered in white cloth. The first woman carried a spear. The second woman carried a dish. And the third woman carried a cup that was filled with light. The three women looked at Percivale and Lancelot. Then, the light slowly faded and the women disappeared.

Lancelot and Percivale wondered at this sight. 'What does this mean?' asked Lancelot.

'It is a vision of the Holy Grail,' King Pelles said. 'It is a vision that will come to Camelot. And when you see this

'It is a vision of the Holy Grail,' King Pelles said.

vision, the knights of Camelot will quest for the Holy Grail.'

'But why do we see the vision here and now?' asked Lancelot.

'I am the guardian[51] of this vision,' said King Pelles. 'I am descended from Joseph of Arimathea who brought the Grail to this land. You have come to this castle for a reason – though I do not know why.'

Lancelot and Percivale did not know the meaning of this vision. Percivale spent much time in prayer and wondered about the meaning of the Holy Grail. Lancelot spent much time with the Lady Blanchefleur and Blanchefleur fell in love with him.

Lancelot lies with Blanchefleur

'I must return to Camelot,' Lancelot said to Blanchefleur. But Blanchefleur was sad and did not want to let him go.

They stayed together all that day and all that night. Lancelot gave Blanchefleur a son – though he did not know of this for many years.

Lancelot and Percivale returned to Camelot and told their stories. Lancelot talked and laughed with Guinevere. But he never spoke of Blanchefleur and their secret love, and soon he forgot about her.

10

The Siege Perilous

Empty seats at the Round Table

Many years had passed. New knights had come to Camelot and old knights had died. Some knights died in quests and others died in battle. There were now empty seats at the Round Table.

Sir Bedivere and Sir Bors sat on Arthur's right. To his left sat Kay and Gareth. Opposite him sat Lancelot and Percivale and Gawain. But there was an empty seat on either side of Gawain and an empty seat beside Sir Bors.

'Who shall sit in these empty places?' asked Arthur. And he looked at the Siege Perilous which had been empty for twenty-four years. No man had ever dared to sit on the Siege Perilous because of Merlin's warning – '*He who sits on this chair will die.*'

Mordred and Galahad

At Whitsun, the holy hermit Naciens returned to Camelot. He brought a young man who was nearly sixteen years old.

Morgana Le Fey also brought a young man to Camelot. Morgana wore the clothes of a holy woman. Her head was covered so that no man could see her face.

Naciens the hermit spoke to Arthur. 'I am Naciens of Carbonek. I bring a squire to your court. I hope he will become a knight. His name is Galahad. I have raised him as my own son. I do not know his father and mother. King Pelles sent him to me when he was a few days old.'

Galahad had a fair and open face. He looked like Lancelot. But Lancelot was worldly and proud. Galahad looked more like a priest than a knight – a quiet young man with a bright and peaceful smile. Galahad was the son of Lancelot by Blanchefleur of Carbonek – though no one knew this secret.

Then the nun, whose face was hidden, stepped forward. 'I am Morgana of Glastonbury,' she said to Arthur. 'I bring a squire to your court. I hope he will become a knight. His name is Mordred.'

Mordred was short and dark and broad. He had the body of a bear and a friendly smile – a smile that masked his evil mind. Men liked him at once. They said that he reminded them of King Arthur.

Arthur had never known his father. He did not know that Mordred looked like Uther Pendragon. And he did not know that Mordred was his own son by Morgana. Also, he did not know that Morgana of Glastonbury was his own half-sister.

Morgana Le Fey brings evil to Camelot

Morgana Le Fey knew most of Merlin's secrets. She was the wisest woman in the world. But her magic had no power over Arthur. While Arthur wore the sword Excalibur, Morgana could not touch him with her magic. But Morgana still had the power to make trouble in the court.

The Knights of the Round Table stood up and welcomed Galahad and Mordred. 'We need young men,' said Bors. 'Welcome to Camelot.'

All the knights and ladies walked and talked in the hall. Then it was time for the feast. 'Be seated, knights and ladies,' said Arthur. 'And let our new squires take a seat at the Round Table. There are two empty places.'

Then Morgana worked her magic of confusion. The knights and ladies took their places, talking and laughing with joy. They paid no attention to the new squires Mordred and Galahad.

Mordred spoke to Galahad. 'There is an empty place on either side of Sir Gawain,' he said. 'Please sit on Sir Gawain's right and I will sit on his left.'

'You are very kind,' said Galahad. 'I thank you.' And Mordred smiled an evil smile.

Galahad sits on the Siege Perilous

All the knights and ladies sat down at the table. And only then did Arthur see that something was wrong. There were no empty places opposite him at the table. No man had dared to sit in the Siege Perilous for twenty-four years. But now Galahad sat in the chair and it was no longer empty.

The second vision of the Holy Grail

As Arthur saw this, there came the sound of a great bell from above the earth. Then music came, from high above, together with the sound of voices singing. The hall was filled with light and the knights and ladies looked at one another in astonishment. Then three ladies came into the hall. They were dressed in white and their faces were covered with white cloth. The first woman carried a spear. The second woman carried a dish. And the third woman carried a cup that was filled with light.

The light was so bright that the knights and ladies could not see the cup. But they were filled with joy and peace. They looked at the cup in wonder. Only Mordred hid his eyes in his hands. He could not look upon the holy cup and he wept. Mordred was unworthy.

A voice spoke softly and clearly. 'Seek the Grail. Only the purest knights can find the Grail.'

The vision faded and all the men and women in the hall were silent and astonished. They looked at King Arthur.

The quest

Arthur spoke. 'Who will seek the Grail?' he asked. 'This is the highest and holiest quest that has come to Camelot. Perhaps it will be the final quest of many knights. Seek the Grail for the honour of Logres and the Glory of God.'

11

The Quest for the Holy Grail

Bedivere and Mordred remain in Camelot

And so the Knights of the Round Table left Camelot. 'We will seek the Holy Grail, for the honour of our King and the Glory of God,' they declared.

Arthur stayed at Camelot with Bedivere and Mordred. All the other Knights of the Round Table set out to seek the Holy Grail.

Bedivere was wounded and had the use of only one hand. So Mordred offered to care for him and to serve the king at court.

Mordred soon learnt about all the rooms in the palace. He knew all the passages and gardens and hallways. He talked to the ladies of the court and heard all their gossip. He talked to the servants and learned all the secrets of the palace.

Months passed. Knights returned to Camelot with news and then set out again in search of the Holy Grail. They searched the Kingdom of Logres for news or for signs of the holy cup. Some knights never returned. They sought the Grail through dark forests and across wild hills and in deep valleys. They fought with wolves and ogres. Knights fell and were lost with no one to tell their story.

'Camelot is empty,' Mordred said to King Arthur. 'We must not lose the traditions of Camelot. We need young knights who can serve the King, the Round Table and the Kingdom of Logres. We need more young knights.'

Arthur listened to Mordred and made new knights. But the young knights quickly became loyal[52] to Mordred and not to Arthur.

Sir Bedivere was silent. He guarded King Arthur and watched and waited.

The Grail Chapel in the Wild Wood

Meanwhile, after many adventures, five knights came together in the Wild Wood near the Castle of Carbonek. Gawain and Bors met Galahad and Percivale and they were joined by Lancelot.

Naciens, the holy hermit of Carbonek, came to them out of the Wild Wood.

'The end of the quest is near. The Chapel of the Grail is hidden in the Wild Wood,' he said. 'Take King Pelles from his castle. Carry him through the wood and you will find the Grail Chapel.'

The five knights went to Castle Carbonek where King Pelles lay on his bed. 'I am in great pain,' said King Pelles. 'The wound that will not heal is painful. You must carry me to the Chapel of the Grail.'

The five knights carried King Pelles on their shields. They went into the Wild Wood and followed a narrow path. The Lady Blanchefleur walked behind them, but she did not speak to Lancelot or Galahad.

Only worthy knights may enter the Grail Chapel

Night fell. The knights walked through the Wild Wood and found their way by moonlight. There were noises in the wood and strange lights and ghostly shapes. At last the knights came to a place where the trees did not grow. A white chapel appeared in the moonlight.

'Carry me into the chapel,' said King Pelles. 'I will be healed there.'

The knights carried him to the chapel door but they could

not enter. Lancelot, Gawain and Bors pushed at the door but it did not open. Then Galahad and Percivale put their hands on the door and the door opened.

Percivale and Galahad carried the wounded king into the chapel. The Lady Blanchefleur entered the chapel with them. But Lancelot, Gawain and Bors could only watch from the doorway. They could not enter because they were not worthy or pure enough.

The third vision of the Holy Grail

The light inside the chapel grew brighter. Percivale and Galahad carried the wounded king to the altar.

Music could be heard from above. It was the music of angels singing. Then three women, dressed in white, appeared in the chapel. The first woman carried a spear. The second woman carried a dish. And the third woman carried a cup that was filled with light. They carried the spear, the dish and the cup to the altar.

Galahad went to the altar. He took the spear and handed it to Percivale. 'Heal the king's wound with this spear,' he said.

Percivale took the spear and touched it to the thigh of King Pelles. The wound was healed at last.

King Pelles sighed. 'I have been the Guardian of the Grail for many years,' he said. 'Now my wound is healed and my task is ended. I hand this task to you, Percivale. I ask you to care for the chapel and my daughter. Now I will rest.'

Then King Pelles fell into a deep sleep and did not wake again in this world. Percivale took Blanchefleur's hand and they looked at Galahad.

Galahad drinks from the Grail and passes from this world

Galahad took the Grail from the altar and raised it to his lips. He drank from the cup and the light grew brighter. The roof of the chapel opened and the light of heaven shone down. Galahad looked upwards and put his hands together in prayer. Then, as the others watched, Galahad rose up into the light.

Those who saw this sight were filled with peace and joy. Then, when the light faded and the music ended, the knights took the body of King Pelles outside. They buried the king at the door of the Grail Chapel.

The guardians of the Grail Chapel

Percivale did not return to Camelot. He married Blanchefleur and became King of Carbonek. Percivale and Blanchefleur guarded the Chapel of the Grail and some time later, they had a son called Lohengrin.

Lancelot, Gawain and Bors returned to Camelot and told their story to the court. King Arthur was filled with joy by the story of the Grail. 'This is the greatest achievement of our knights,' he said. 'This story will be told for as long as men tell stories. And while men tell this story, Camelot will never end.'

But Lancelot did not tell all the story. He did say that he could not enter the Grail Chapel. He did not say that he was unworthy. Mordred smiled an evil smile and looked at Lancelot. Lancelot turned his eyes to Guinevere.

12

The Breaking of the Round Table

Mordred's knights at Camelot

Many knights did not return to Camelot. They were lost in the Quest for the Holy Grail. Young knights came to Camelot and soon there was a division in the court. The old knights surrounded King Arthur. The young knights gathered around Mordred.

Mordred said to the young knights, 'King Arthur is old. Soon there will be changes in Camelot. We will have a new king and many things will be different.'

Mordred watched Lancelot and Guinevere closely. He saw them ride together and followed them when they rode into the forest. He watched while they hunted deer together. He told his friends, 'Guinevere is closer to Lancelot than to her husband King Arthur.'

Arthur had heard the rumours, but he refused to believe them. There was peace in the Kingdom of Logres. Arthur was happy to rule wisely and well. He ate and drank at the Round Table. He welcomed many knights and heard their stories, but he no longer rode out in search of adventure. His hair had turned from the colour of gold to the colour of silver.

Mordred spoke to his mother, Morgana Le Fey. 'How can we make Arthur believe that Lancelot and Guinevere are unfaithful[53] to him?' he asked.

Mordred plots against Lancelot and Guinevere

'There is a secret garden in the woods,' said Morgana Le Fey. 'Lancelot and Guinevere meet there. I will put a magic spell on the garden so that Lancelot and Guinevere fall asleep. When they are asleep, you will fetch Arthur and show him that his wife and his champion knight are lovers.'

Mordred watched and waited. He saw Lancelot and Guinevere ride out of Camelot. It was the month of May and the road was covered with white flowers. The knight and the queen rode into the wood. They came to the secret garden and sat down on the grass among the flowers. Suddenly they felt tired and soon they were asleep – lying side by side.

Lancelot and Guinevere in the secret garden

Mordred rode back to Camelot and went to the King. 'Sire,' he said, 'I saw two horses in the wood. The horses had no riders and they are the horses of Sir Lancelot and Our Lady Queen. Perhaps they have fallen or some accident has happened...'

So Arthur rode into the wood. Mordred led him to the secret garden. There Arthur saw Lancelot and Guinevere asleep on the grass among the flowers. They had their arms around each other.

As Arthur drew his sword Excalibur, Mordred smiled an evil smile. 'I will kill this false knight,' said Arthur. Then, as he raised his sword to kill Sir Lancelot, Merlin's words came into his mind.

'You will not draw the sword Excalibur in anger. You will draw that sword only to defend the right. And, while you fight for good against evil, you cannot fall in battle. The sword will protect you and you will defend the land.'

Arthur drove the sword into the ground next to Sir Lancelot's head. Then he turned away and rode back to Camelot. Mordred went with him and told everyone what had happened in the wood. Soon all the court knew that Lancelot and Guinevere had been unfaithful to their lord the King.

Lancelot and Guinevere escape from Camelot

Soon Lancelot and Guinevere awoke in the secret garden. They saw the sword Excalibur and cried out in terror. 'Arthur!' Guinevere cried. 'What shall we do? Where shall we hide?'

'Take the sword Excalibur,' said Lancelot. 'No man has ever touched it except Arthur. Take it and keep it until the King needs it for battle.'

Then Lancelot took Guinevere away into the west. 'We have sinned[54] badly,' he said. 'We have been unfaithful to our lord the King. Now we must part forever. We cannot go back to Camelot and we cannot go forward together.'

Guinevere enters a nunnery

Lancelot took Guinevere to the nunnery at Amesbury in the West Country. Guinevere carried the sword Excalibur with her for the King's great need. There the women took the queen into their nunnery and she became a nun. 'Shut me behind high walls,' she said, 'so that no man may see my sin and shame.' And so she lived in a simple room and spent her days in prayer. But she kept the sword Excalibur hidden in her room. It was her last service to her king and husband.

Lancelot becomes a hermit

Lancelot rode into the west. He left his armour and sword at a church and became a hermit. He lived alone in the woods and never spoke to anyone again.

Mordred makes war against Arthur

Meanwhile, Mordred gathered the young knights around him. 'Arthur has lost his power,' he said. 'It is time we had a new king – a young king. The Round Table is old and powerless.

We will fight the old knights and there will be a new beginning in this land.'

And so there was war in the land for the first time since the Battle of Badon Hill. Mordred and the young knights attacked Camelot. Sir Gawain and Sir Bors led the old knights out of the castle and they battled with Mordred on the banks of the river.

'Where is Arthur?' Mordred called. 'Is he afraid to fight us?'

Arthur sat in his great hall. He sat at the Round Table with his faithful knight Sir Bedivere. 'The Round Table is broken,' he said. 'We shall never see such a gathering of noble knights again.'

Gawain and Bors pushed Mordred's men back to the river. Morgana Le Fey helped her son by sending confusion among the knights. But the spell confused Mordred's men as well and Mordred had to call them back.

The death of Gawain and Bors

Bors fell on the bridge across the river. Many men died on that bridge. They fell into the river and their bodies floated to the sea.

Before he left the battlefield, Mordred rode behind Gawain who fought alone. Mordred swung his black war axe and split Gawain's helmet. Gawain fell from his horse and died in a field close to Camelot.

Mordred took his men and destroyed the lands to the west. He burned the towns and villages. He killed many men, women and children. And his army grew larger. He promised his men, 'You can keep what you can take.' And his men robbed and burned the countryside. They were like the invaders from across the sea who came before Arthur's time.

Then Morgana, his mother, spoke and said, 'Arthur has lost

the sword Excalibur. He will look for it in the West Country. I know where the sword came from. We will go to the place and wait. It is a place of power. I will be strong there. Arthur will come. We will fight him, and that will be Arthur's end.'

Arthur gathered all his men and rode after Sir Mordred. Mordred moved west and Arthur followed. Slowly they moved ever further west. Winter came and still they moved ever more slowly towards the land of the sunset.

Guinevere gives Excalibur to Arthur

Arthur came at night to the holy house at Amesbury. The nuns admitted him to Guinevere's cell. Guinevere could not speak or look at Arthur. She took the sword Excalibur from beneath her simple bed and handed it to the king.

'You are the only person to touch this sword,' said Arthur. 'Since the time I took it from the Lady of the Lake, no other person has held it. Remember me, and may we meet again in another life. Then, I pray, we shall know each other for the first time.'

And so he left the nunnery and Guinevere remained. She lived out her days as a nun and never spoke again.

Merlin comes to Arthur in his sleep

Arthur pushed Sir Mordred back to the land's end. They passed through deep forests where the sun barely shone. They came to bare hills where no man lived and nothing grew.

From these hills, Arthur saw a valley and a lake in the far west. Beyond the lake lay a plain of sand. Beyond the plain of sand lay the ocean and, far off, distant islands where the sun sets. Here, Mordred could go no further and he and Arthur prepared for their final battle.

Arthur rested that night beside the cold and misty lake. Far away, in the middle of the great wood, Merlin woke for a short time from his long sleep. And Merlin's voice came to Arthur in a dream and spoke of Excalibur and the Lady of the Lake. 'One day you must give it back to her,' he had said. And Arthur had asked: 'How shall I know that day?' 'You will know that day when you come to this lake again,' Merlin had answered. 'Now, it is time for battle.'

And Merlin came to Morgana in her sleep. 'Remember the dragon,' he said. So Morgana rose and prepared her spells to defend her son against her brother.

And Merlin also came to Lancelot in his sleep. 'Take your sword and go to your king,' he said. So Lancelot rose and took his sword from the church and rode into the west.

The last battle in the West

Arthur rose and prepared for battle. He prepared to fight Mordred on the plain of sand. Then a strange mist came over the sand. It was the last day of the old year. It was a cold day and the sun was dim. Soon the mist covered the sand and no man could see the sun.

Morgana used her magic. She called the mist from out of the lake, and she sent confusion among the knights. All day long they fought and even Arthur was confused. Men could not see each other clearly in the mist. They fought against shadows and killed friends as well as enemies.

Then the winter sunlight broke through the mist and a knight appeared. His sword shone in the gleam of sunlight. It was Lancelot. He charged at Mordred's men and drove them back towards the ocean shore. The mist cleared for a moment and Arthur's men charged forward.

Morgana saw that Lancelot was winning the battle. She spoke words of great power. It was the most powerful spell she had ever spoken. It was the spell that gave her the breath of the dragon. She breathed in the face of Arthur's men, even as Lancelot prepared to kill Mordred.

Lancelot was driven backwards by the breath of the dragon. Mordred leapt forward and swung his black war axe. Lancelot fell and died on the plain of sand. And all around him men fought on in the mist.

But the dragon spell was too powerful for Morgana. She breathed fire and it burned her. She fell to the ground and was covered with fire. All her evil burned in the fire and she died.

The death of Mordred

The mist cleared. The field was filled with dead knights. Arthur stood alone with Sir Bedivere. Bedivere could not fight because of his wounded hand. All the other Knights of the Round Table were dead. And all the enemies of Arthur were dead except for Mordred.

Mordred walked across the bloody field towards King Arthur. He carried his black war axe and Arthur held the sword Excalibur.

Arthur and Mordred fought as the sun sank low in the west. And Arthur drove his sword Excalibur into the body of Mordred and killed him. But, before he fell, Mordred swung his black war axe and struck King Arthur on the head.

The Passing of Arthur

Arthur returns Excalibur to the Lady of the Lake

Sir Bedivere carried King Arthur to a chapel that stood on a narrow strip of land. On one side lay the lake and on the other lay the ocean. The moon was full.

'I shall die before the morning,' said King Arthur. 'Take my sword Excalibur and throw it into the lake.'

Sir Bedivere took the sword, sadly, and walked to the lake. He looked at the sword and saw that it was beautiful. 'It is too good to throw away,' he thought. And so he hid the sword in the grass beside the lake and walked back to the wounded king.

'What did you see?' Arthur whispered.

'Nothing,' said Sir Bedivere.

'Go again and do as I told you,' said King Arthur.

Sir Bedivere went to the lake a second time and looked at the sword. 'Who will remember King Arthur when this sword is lost?' he thought. And so he hid the sword a second time.

'What did you see?' Arthur whispered. His voice was becoming weaker.

'Nothing,' said Sir Bedivere.

Then Arthur was angry. 'Does no one obey a dying king?' he asked. 'Now, on your honour, go and do what I told you. This is my last request and final command.'

Then Bedivere went quickly to the lake. He took the sword and closed his eyes and threw Excalibur into the middle of the lake. When he looked, he saw the sword flash in the moonlight and fall towards the water. But the sword did not sink into the lake. A hand rose from the water. The hand was covered in white cloth. The hand caught the sword and waved it three times. Then the Lady of the Lake pulled the sword beneath the water.

Bedivere ran back to the wounded king. Arthur looked at Bedivere's face. 'I know that you have done what I commanded,' he said. 'Now carry me to the ocean shore, but be quick. I fear that I shall die.'

Three queens carry Arthur to Avalon

Bedivere carried Arthur to the ocean shore. A boat appeared in the moonlight. It moved without wind, sails or oars. Three queens stood in the boat. It was decorated with rich red cloth. Bedivere laid Arthur on a bed of rich red cushions. The three queens wept.

'Where will you go?' Sir Bedivere asked.

Arthur answered slowly. 'I am going a long way with these women. I am going to the island valley of Avalon. It is an isle of rest where winter never comes. There I will be healed of my wound and will rest and wait. And one day I shall come again, for Merlin called me the Once and Future King.'

'And where shall I go?' asked Sir Bedivere.

'You shall travel through the world,' said Arthur. 'You shall tell of what you saw and what you heard – the stories of the Knights of the Round Table. The stories shall be told until the ending of the world.'

Then the three queens sang a sad song as the boat moved away from the shore. The boat gleamed in the moonlight.

The last of the Knights

Bedivere walked back to the cold bare hills. From the hills he looked across the water. He saw the boat. It was small but bright. The boat moved slowly towards the islands in the west.

The sword reads: *Cast me away*

'The stories shall be told until the ending of the world.'

The islands were lost in the darkness of night. But the boat gleamed in the last light of the frosty moon.

Bedivere watched for a long time. The moon faded. Behind him, dawn broke. Bedivere saw the last gleam of Arthur's boat in the first light of day. He heard a great shout of many voices, and then the gleam was gone.

The hills were bare but bright as Bedivere began to walk towards the east. And the sun rose on a new day.

Points For Understanding

1

1 The army of Uther attacked Tintagel Castle. What did the army of Uther do exactly?
2 How was Uther able to enter Tintagel Castle?

2

1 Who were Arthur's parents and why did he live with Sir Ector?
2 How did Arthur become King of Britain?

3

1 What was the difference between the Sword of Right and the Sword of Might?
2 How will Arthur know when to return Excalibur to the lake?

4

1 Lancelot was the Champion Knight of Camelot. Explain the meaning of the word 'champion' in the story.
2 Merlin and Nimuë spoke to each other without words. How did they speak to each other?

5

1 What did Nimuë and Morgana want from Merlin?
2 'You must rule without my help.' Why did Merlin say this to Arthur?

6

1 Why are these things important in this chapter?
  (a) an axe (b) a bargain (c) a green ribbon

7

1 What curse did the sorceress put on Sir Meliot?
2 What curse did the sorceress put on Elaine?

8

1 Explain the importance of the love potion in this story.
2 'I see a black sail,' said Iseult of the White Hands. Why did she say this?

9

1 Why did Sir Kay laugh at Sir Percivale?
2 What was the Holy Grail?

10

1 What was the Siege Perilous?
2 Mordred wanted Galahad to sit on the Siege Perilous. Why?
3 Why could Mordred not look at the holy cup?

11

1 Why did Mordred not go on the quest?
2 Why could Lancelot not enter the Grail Chapel?

12

1 Why did Morgana Le Fey put a spell on the secret garden in the forest?
2 Where did Arthur fight his last battle?
3 How did Morgana die?

13

1 Why did Sir Bedivere not want to cast Excalibur into the lake?
2 Where did Arthur go?

Glossary

1 **warrior** (page 4)
an old word for a soldier.
2 **invader** – *to invade* (page 4)
if you invade a country you take or send an army into it in order to get control of it. The people who do this are called *invaders*.
3 **empire** (page 4)
a number of countries that are ruled by one person or government.
4 **attacked** – *to attack* (page 4)
to use violence against a person or place.
5 **court** (page 5)
the place where a king or queen lives and works. Someone who has an official position at the *court* of a king or queen, or who spends time there, is a *courtier*.
6 **magician** (page 5)
someone who uses magic to make impossible things happen. A man in stories who has magic powers is also called a *wizard*. A woman who uses evil spirits to do magic in stories is called a *sorceress*.
7 **chivalrous** (page 5)
polite and kind behaviour by men towards women.
8 **honour, truth and justice** (page 5)
These were the things that the knights believed in. *Honour* is the respect that people have for someone who achieves something great, is very powerful, or behaves in a way that is morally right. *Truth* is the quality of being true, and someone who says what is true and does not lie *speaks truthfully*. *Justice* is treatment of people that is fair and morally right, and someone who is fair and morally right is *just*.
9 **quest** (page 5)
a long difficult search
10 **raven** (page 9)
a large bird with shiny black feathers.
11 **blow** (page 9)
a hard hit from someone's hand or an object. If you *strike someone*, you hit someone or something with your hand, a tool, or a weapon. You can also say *strike (someone) a blow*. A hit made with someone's hand, a stick, or another object is also called a *stroke*.

12 **swan** (page 9)
   a large white bird with a long neck that lives near water.
13 **Sire** (page 10)
   an old word used for talking to a king. There are a lot of words
   used before people's names in this book. *Sir* is used before the name
   of a man who is a knight. *Lord* is used before the name of a man
   who has a high rank in the highest British social class. *Lady* is used
   as a title for some women who have important social or official
   positions.
14 **protect** (page 11)
   to keep someone or something safe.
15 **spell** (page 11)
   words or actions that are believed to make magic things happen.
   If you *cast a spell*, you use magic to make something happen to
   someone, or to seem to do this. If you *break a spell*, you end it. *Spells*
   can make good or bad things happen. If you *curse* someone, you use
   magic powers to make bad things happen to someone. These bad
   things are called a *curse*.
16 **wound** (page 12)
   an injury in which your skin or flesh is seriously damaged. Someone
   who is seriously injured is *wounded*.
17 **gave birth** – *to give birth (to someone)* (page 13)
   to produce a baby from inside your body. A baby that is recently
   born is *newborn*.
18 **nunnery** (page 13)
   a place where religious women – or *nuns* – live together.
19 **archbishop** (page 14)
   a priest of the highest rank in some Christian churches.
20 **astonished** (page 16)
   very surprised.
21 **sign** (page 19)
   a piece of evidence that something exists or is happening.
22 **plenty** (page 21)
   a situation in which large supplies of something are available,
   especially food.
23 **deed** (page 22)
   a literary word meaning something that someone does.
24 **ogre** (page 23)
   a cruel frightening person.

25 **heir** (page 23)

someone who will receive money, property, or a title when another person dies.

26 **squire** (page 25)

a young man in the Middle Ages who worked for a knight and carried his shield. Squires wanted to become knights.

27 **sorceress** (page 26)

a woman who uses evil spirits to do magic in stories.

28 **half-sister** (page 27)

a sister who has either the same mother or the same father as you have.

29 **abbey** (page 28)

a large church with buildings connected to it for monks or nuns to live in. An *abbess* is a woman who is in charge of a convent (a religious community of women).

30 **Joseph of Arimathea** (page 28)

in the Christian bible, a rich man who was a supporter of Jesus.

31 **heal** (page 28)

if an injury heals, or if someone heals it, the skin or bone grows back together and becomes healthy again. Someone who can cure people who are ill, using special powers that other people do not understand, is called a *healer*.

32 **joust** (page 29)

a competition between two people riding horses. They fight by riding towards each other and trying to hit each other with a long stick called a *lance*.

33 **noble** (page 32)

behaving in a brave and honest way that other people admire.

34 **challenge** (page 33)

if you *challenge* someone, you invite them to compete or fight. This invitation is called a *challenge*.

35 **bargain** (page 35)

an agreement in which each person or group promises something.

36 **maiden** (page 37)

an old word meaning a girl or young woman who is not married. *Maid* has the same meaning.

37 **ribbon** (page 37)

a long narrow piece of coloured cloth or paper that is used for decorating or tying things.

38 *companion* (page 43)
someone who is with you or who you spend a lot of time with.

39 *tapestry* (page 44)
a thick heavy cloth that has pictures or patterns woven into it.

40 *minstrel* (page 46)
a singer or musician who travelled and performed at the time of King Arthur.

41 *harp* (page 46)
a musical instrument that consists of a row of strings stretched over a large upright frame.

42 *pirate* (page 48)
someone who steals things from ships while they are sailing.

43 *dragon* (page 49)
in stories, an imaginary large animal that breathes out fire.

44 *claws* (page 50)
one of the sharp curved nails that some birds and animals have on their feet.

45 *potion* (page 51)
a drink that is believed to be magic, poisonous, or useful as a medicine. A *love potion* is believed to make the person who drinks it fall in love.

46 *buried* – *to bury* (page 55)
to put something in the ground and cover it with earth.

47 *grave* (page 55)
the place where a dead person is buried in a deep hole under the ground.

48 *unworthy* (page 57)
a *worthy* person has qualities that make people respect them. An *unworthy* person lacks these qualities.

49 *hermit* (page 58)
someone who chooses to live alone, or someone who spends most of their time alone.

50 *vision* (page 59)
something that someone sees in a dream or as a religious experience.

51 *guardian* (page 61)
a person who protects something.

52 *loyal* (page 66)
someone who is loyal continues to support a person or organisation.

53 ***unfaithful*** (page 70)

having a sexual relationship with someone who is not your husband, wife or usual partner.

54 ***sin*** *– to sin* (page 72)

if you *sin*, you do something that is wrong according to religious laws. You commit a *sin*.

Exercises

Vocabulary: words in the story

Choose the best word in the following sentences.

> **Example:**   The servant put ~~sugar~~ / ~~water~~ / poison / ~~spice~~ into
> Uther's wine. Uther drank the wine and died.

1 His eyes were the colour of the clear blue sea / sky / pond / shore.

2 'Winter is coming and my men have little feet / mouth / sword / food.'

3 Uther promised / ordered / told / remembered to give the child,
Arthur, to Merlin.

4 'We will have a feast / contest / battle / prayer to see who can pull the
sword from the stone.'

5 The people attacked / invaded / played / suffered because there was no
order in the land.

6 'Father, put your sword back in its box / sheath / container / holder,'
Arthur said.

7 The sword from the stone is a sign / warning / notice / word that you
are king.

8 Arthur fought six battles and won / lost / defeated / invaded his
enemies.

9 It was a time of peace and plenty / party / poetry / pretty and the
people were happy.

10 'The empty seat is called the Chair / Stool / Siege / Bench Perilous,'
said Merlin.

11 You may strike the first go / axe / sword / blow and I will strike the
second.

12 'Gawain has made a terrible bargain / break / choice / permit,' thought
the Knights.

13 It is Christmas – a time of peace and party / luck / celebration / feast.

14 'I <u>look / search / quest / seek</u> the Green Chapel and the Green Knight,' said Gawain.

---

15 'It is a cold night. Would you like a <u>maiden / ribbon / guest / squire</u> of the castle to visit you?'

---

16 'I have a gift for you – a piece of green ribbon. The ribbon will <u>protect / warm / thank / present</u> you.'

---

17 Sir Gawain did not <u>keep / make / break / take</u> his promise to the Green Knight.

---

18 'I have cursed Sir Meliot. Now his wound will never <u>better / heal / bleed / mark</u>.'

---

19 No man has gone into the Chapel Perilous and returned <u>at once / in time / arrive / alive</u>.

---

20 'If Iseult the Fair comes, raise a white <u>flag / sign / sail / sheet</u> on your ship.'

---

21 Mordred could not look at the holy cup because he was <u>ugly / blind / short / unworthy</u>.

---

22 The words on the sword were TAKE ME UP and <u>throw / pull / draw / cast</u> ME AWAY.

Writing: rewrite sentences

Use words from the box to rewrite these sentences. You may need to make some changes, such as verb tenses. There are two extra words.

~~army~~ wounds food hermit Champion swords and axes
companion drive messengers raise gift battle squire
deeds potion nunnery goat-herd guardian fall protect
white quest

Example: *Uther was a strong king with <u>a lot of soldiers</u>.*
You write: *Uther was a strong king with a large army.*

1 Merlin's hair was <u>the colour of snow</u>.

   Merlin's hair

2 Winter is coming and my men have <u>few supplies</u>.

   Winter is coming

3 'I will <u>keep you safe</u>,' said Merlin.

   I will

4 The armies of Uther and Gorloïs fought with <u>weapons</u>.

   The armies of

5 His body was covered in blood from many <u>cuts</u>.

   His body was

6 'I will send <u>people with messages</u> through all the lands of Britain.'

   I will send

7 He <u>lifted</u> the sword above his head and the metal flashed brightly in the sunlight.

   He

8 Excalibur is a <u>present</u> from the Lady of the Lake.

   Excalibur is a

9 You will fight many <u>fights between armies</u>.

   You will

10 The knights of Camelot did many great and good <u>actions</u>.

The knights
___

11 Two <u>young men who were going to be knights</u> held the knights' horses.

Two
___

12 Uther put Morgana into <u>a place where holy women live</u>.

Uther put Morgana
___

13 Tristram and Iseult drank the love <u>drink</u>.

Tristram and Iseult
___

14 Lancelot was the <u>First Knight</u> of Camelot.

Lancelot was
___

15 Percivale <u>looked after his family's goats</u>.

Percivale
___

16 The knights of Camelot will <u>go and look for</u> the Holy Grail.

The knights
___

17 'I am the <u>person who looks after</u> the Grail,' said King Pelles.

I am the
___

18 Bors <u>was killed in battle</u> on the bridge across the river.

Bors
___

19 Arthur <u>pushed his sword hard</u> into the body of Mordred.

Arthur
___

Grammar: comparisons with as ... as ...

Use the words in the box. Look at the example. Can you make similar comparisons?

~~snow~~   death   grass   sky   night   bear   blood   sun   stone

Example: *Merlin's hair was white.*
You write: *Merlin's hair was as white as snow.*

1 Uther Pendragon was strong.

_____

2 The strange knight's beard was green.

_____

3 Arthur's eyes were blue.

_____

4 Lancelot's rose was red.

_____

5 The ice on the hills was hard.

_____

6 The smoke was black.

_____

7 The light was bright.

_____

8 Sir Meliot was pale.

_____

_____

Grammar & Vocabulary: just

The knights of Camelot fight for truth, honour and *justice*. King Arthur is a noble and *just* king. But you will often hear the word JUST in spoken English with a different meaning.

NOUN JUSTICE	ADJECTIVE of justice JUST	ADVERB JUST
treatment of people that is fair and right	good and fair	1. a short time ago 2. only, simply

Is the word JUST used as an adjective or an adverb in the following sentences?

		ADJ	ADV
1	Bedivere was a just and honest man.		
2	Lancelot arrived just in time during the battle.		
3	There were just a few knights left in Camelot during the quest.		
4	Uther Pendragon was not a just and honourable king.		

Can you use the adverb JUST in the following sentences?
Look at the examples.

Example 1:	*We have now finished. (We finished a minute ago.)*
You write:	*We've just finished.*

Example 2:	*It only takes a few minutes.*
You write:	*It takes just a few minutes. / It just takes a few minutes.*

5 You simply press the button marked SEND.

_____

6 There are three buttons, but you only press the button marked SEND.

_____

_____

94

7 It will be ready in a very short time.

8 I was only wondering if you'd like to go.

9 I found you barely in time.

Vocabulary choice: words which are related in meaning

Which word is most closely related? Look at the example then try to match the rest.

Example:	sword	speech	<u>weapon</u>	swear	armour
1	gold	ancient	colour	bear	jewel
2	besiege	surround	defend	attend	descend
3	spell	time	place	wisdom	magic
4	poison	medicine	healthy	murder	fish
5	cathedral	castle	palace	church	minstrel
6	astonished	amazed	bored	successful	founded
7	might	worth	weakness	volume	power
8	deeds	laws	arms	exercises	actions
9	perilous	safe	possible	dangerous	attractive
10	stroke	hit	fire	meat	boat
11	quest	answer	search	host	reply
12	celebration	festival	decoration	occasional	assembly
13	ribbon	band	clothing	metal	wood
14	curse	speak evil	speak well	say prayers	talk badly
15	maid	done	girl	cook	taken

Macmillan Education
4 Crinan Street
London N1 9XW
A division of Macmillan Publishers Limited
Companies and representatives throughout the world

ISBN 978–0–230–03444–0
ISBN 978–0–230–02685–8 (with CD pack)

This version of *King Arthur and the Knights of The Round Table* was
retold by Stephen Colbourn for Macmillan Readers

First published 2008
Text © Macmillan Publishers Limited 2008
Design and illustration © Macmillan Publishers Limited 2008
This version first published 2008

Illustrated by Janos Jantner and Martin Sanders
Cover image by Getty Images/Look

Printed and bound in Great Britain by Ashford Colour Press Ltd

2019   2018   2017
15   14   13   12   11   10   9   8

with CD pack
2019   2018   2017
15   14   13   12   11   10   9   8